A General Equilibrium Study

of the Monetary Mechanism

David L. Schulze

A UNIVERSITY OF FLORIDA BOOK

THE UNIVERSITY PRESSES OF FLORIDA

GAINESVILLE / 1974

Library of Congress Cataloging in Publication Data

Schulze, David. 1939—
    A general equilibrium study of the monetary mechanism.

    (University of Florida social sciences monograph no. 51)
    "A University of Florida book."
    Bibliography: p.
    1. Money supply. 2. Equilibrium (Economics).
    3. Money supply — Mathematical models. I. Title.
    II. Series: Florida. University, Gainesville.
    University of Florida monographs. Social sciences, no. 51.
    HG221.S358   332.4   74–13495
    ISBN 0–8130–0407–1

PRINTED BY BOYD BROTHERS, INCORPORATED
PANAMA CITY, FLORIDA

Acknowledgments

I SHOULD like to express my appreciation to the National Science Foundation for providing funds to support this work and to Iowa State University for actually allocating the funds under the NSF grant.

I am also deeply indebted to Professor Dudley G. Luckett for his guidance throughout the course of the project. Special thanks go to my wife for her cheerful suffering of the effects of my frustrations.

Thanks must go also to the Graduate School of the University of Florida for making possible the publication of this monograph.

William E. Carter

Contents

1. Review of the Literature

THE CLASSICAL dichotomy between the real and monetary variables in the economy is, in one form or another, an extremely hardy beast. One of its milder reincarnations is the idea that an examination of the determinants of the stock of money is, at best, only an intellectual game, since the chain of causality runs from income and prices to the money stock. The demand for money is visualized as primarily a function of the level of national income, and any correlation between income and prices and money is due solely to the "pull" of income on the money stock.[1] No important feedback from the money stock to income and prices is believed to exist.

With the great deal of work done in the 1950s and early 1960s providing a convincing theoretical basis for the existence of a chain of causality running from the money stock to the real variables in the economy,[2] not to mention Keynes' work (31, 32), economists began, in the early 1960s, to investigate more thoroughly the determination of the money stock. The forces affecting the money stock were important, since the money stock in turn affected the level of prices and income.

The primary purpose of this work is to examine the processes through which the money stock is determined. In addition, further theoretical support will be provided for the position that changes in the stock of money affect the level of economic activity, and the effects and effectiveness of the various tools of monetary policy will be examined. The framework in which this will be carried out is a general equilibrium model of the economy composed of five sectors—the public, manufacturing firms, banks, nonbank financial firms, and the government.

1. See, for example, Goldsmith (26) and Klein and Goldberger (33). Full information on literature cited begins on p. 151. For definitions of symbols used in the model, see Appendix, p. 145.

2. Patinkin's *Money, Interest, and Prices* (47) served as both a milestone and a stimulus for further work in this area.

1

This work is primarily an extension of what is commonly referred to as "money supply theory." The basic idea of the approaches to be discussed is to generate expressions for the stock of money in terms of the variables of whatever economic model is postulated, and to derive statements about the effects of changes in these variables on the stock of money. These expressions for the money stock are called money supply equations.[3]

The study of the supply of money began with the early work of C. A. Phillips (48) and others (1, 35, 39, 50) in the 1920s and 1930s. Their work culminated in the standard textbook money multipliers, with which we are so familiar, like $\Delta M = (1/r)$ times the original change in the money stock (where r is the average reserve requirement). No real advance in this area occurred until the 1960s and the appearance of the works of Milton Friedman and Anna Schwartz (24), Phillip Cagan (10), and Karl Brunner and Alan Meltzer (4, 5, 6, 8, 41). The Friedman-Schwartz-Cagan and Brunner-Meltzer approaches to the money supply are the best known today.

The Friedman-Schwartz-Cagan[4] approach is based on two simple definitions. The money stock, M, is equal to total currency holdings, C, and total demand deposits:

$$M = C + D. \tag{1.1}$$

High-powered money, H, defined as the total of all types of money that can be used as currency or reserves, is simply

$$H = C + R \tag{1.2}$$

where R is simply reserves.

The basic Friedman-Schwartz-Cagan result is obtained by simply divid-

---

3. They are not supply equations in the normal sense of the term, since they all purport to give the actual stock of money when the values of their parameters are known. If they were true supply equations, the actual stock of money would be given, not by the "supply" equation alone, but by simultaneous solution of the aggregate demand for money equation and a "true" supply equation. For this reason, we choose to speak of the monetary mechanism implying a simultaneous determination of the money stock, rather than the supply of money alone.

4. Cagan's tautology for the money stock is slightly different from that presented in Appendix B to *A Monetary History of the U.S., 1867-1960* by Friedman and Schwartz (24). Cagan's formulation is based on the tautology derived by Friedman and Schwartz described in the text.

ing Equation 1.1 by Equation 1.2 which yields, after a few simple algebraic manipulations,[5]

$$M = H \; \frac{D/R \; (1 + D/C)}{D/R + D/C} \; .$$ (1.3)

Equation 1.3 is a tautology, being derived from the definitions of M and H. In this approach the money stock is determined by the decisions of three sectors: the government, which determines H; the public, by determining its deposit to currency ratio, D/C; and the banks, by determining the deposit to reserve ratio, D/R. Friedman and Schwartz (24) call H, D/R, and D/C the "proximate determinants" of the money stock (p. 791). The factors underlying these proximate determinants are spelled out only vaguely. D/C is said to depend upon the "relative usefulness" of deposits and currency, the costs of holding these assets, and "perhaps income" (p. 787). D/R is a function of legal reserve requirements and precautionary reserves (p. 785). The determinants of H are not spelled out specifically, even though a large portion of the book is devoted to describing and analyzing various actions by the monetary authorities.

Brunner and Meltzer actually present two hypotheses—linear and non-linear. Their linear hypothesis is based on the reaction of the banking system to the presence of surplus reserves, defined as the difference between actual and desired reserves, the portfolio adjustments caused by these surplus reserves (4, 8), and the process by which surplus reserves are generated or absorbed.

The total portfolio response of the banking system to the presence of surplus reserves is given by

$$dE = \frac{1}{\lambda - \mu} \; S$$ (1.4)

5. The derivation of Equation 1.3 is: (1) $M/H = C + D/C + R$. Multiplying numerator and denominator by D yields (2) $M/H = DC + D^2/DC + RD$. Then the right-hand side of (2) is multiplied by RC/RC, yielding

$$\frac{M}{H} = \frac{\frac{DC+D^2}{RC}}{\frac{DC+RD}{RC}} = \frac{\frac{DC}{RC} + \frac{D^2}{RC}}{\frac{DC}{RC} + \frac{RD}{RC}} = \frac{\frac{D}{R} + \frac{D^2}{RC}}{\frac{D}{R} + \frac{D}{C}} = \frac{\frac{D}{R} (1 + \frac{D}{C})}{\frac{D}{R} + \frac{D}{C}} \; .$$

Multiplying both sides by H gives the desired result.

where E is the value of the banks' portfolio, S is the amount of surplus reserves, and λ is the average loss coefficient (i.e., λ measures the amount of surplus reserves lost per dollar of portfolio adjustment). λ is less than 1 since the banking system will generate added deposits (and thus reserves) as it attempts to eliminate surplus reserves by buying interest-bearing assets. μ is equal to $(1 - n)p$, where p is the average spillover of deposits from the expanding bank (the one trying to eliminate surplus reserves) to other banks and n is a linear combination of average spillover into currency and time deposits. Thus μ reduces the average loss coefficient and the term $(\lambda - \mu)^{-1}$ is Brunner and Meltzer's money multiplier for responses to surplus reserves. Surplus reserves are given by the relation

$$S = A_o \ dB + dL - A_1 \ dC_o + A_2 \ dt_o + A_3 \ dE - dV_o^d; \qquad (1.5)$$

B is the monetary base (the amount of money issued by the government); L is the total of changes in required reserves resulting from changes in the average reserve requirement and from the redistribution of deposits among various classes of banks; E is a parameter measuring the structure of interbank deposits; dC_o represents changes in the public's demand for currency occurring *independently* of changes in the public's monetary wealth; dt_o represents changes in the public's demand for time deposits occurring *independently* of the public's wealth; and dV_o represents changes in the banks' demand for cash assets in excess of required reserves occurring independently of changes in the level of banks' deposits. The A_i are positive constants. Then the change in M^2 (defined as currency plus demand deposits plus time deposits) is given by

$$dM^2 = m^2 s + q \ dB \qquad (1.6)$$

where m^2 is the surplus reserve (or money) multiplier and q is the proportion of a change in the money base that affects bank reserves and deposits simultaneously.

The change in M^1 $(M^2 - T)$ is

$$dM^1 = m^1 s + q \ dB - dt_o \qquad (1.7)$$

where m^1 is the money multiplier for the definition of M excluding time deposits.

Replacing s in Equations 1.6 and 1.7 with Equation 1.5 and integrating yields the linear hypothesis' expressions for M^1 and M^2:

$$M^2 = m_o + m^2(B + L) - m^2 A_1 C_o + m^2 A_2 t_o - m^2 V_o^d (i) \qquad (1.8)$$

$$M^1 = n_o + m^1(B + L) - m^1 A_1 C_o - [1 - m^1 A_2] t_o -$$
$$m^1 V_o^d(i) \qquad (1.9)$$

where $B + L$ is the "extended monetary base," m_o and n_o are positive constants, and the notation $V_o^d(i)$ is used to express the dependence of the money stock on interest rates through the impact of interest rates on the banks' asset portfolio. m^1 and m^2 are the money multipliers.

Behind the terms C_o, t_o, and V_o lie the public's demands for currency and time deposits, which depend upon the public's money wealth, nonmoney wealth, and all interest rates, as well as the banks' demand for "available cash assets," which depends on the relevant interest rates and the level of deposit liabilities.

Again the money stock depends upon the decision of three sectors: the government in determining $B + L$, the public in determining C_o and t_o, and the banking system in determining V_o^d (i). Implicit in this hypothesis is the assumption, as Fand has pointed out (19), that the marginal propensities to hold time and demand deposits (with respect to changes in M) are constant.

Brunner and Meltzer's nonlinear hypothesis centers on the credit market. The money stock and interest rates emerge from the interaction of the public's supply of assets to the banks and the banks' resulting portfolio readjustment.

The banks' desired rate of portfolio readjustment, $\overset{\circ}{E}{}^s$, is given by

$$\overset{\circ}{E}{}^s = h (R - R^d) \qquad (1.10)$$

where R is actual reserves and R^d is desired reserves.

$$R^d = R^d (D, T, i, \rho) \qquad (1.11)$$

where i is a vector of all interest rates and ρ is the discount rate. Excess reserves, R^e, are given by

$$R^e = R^e (i, \rho, D + T). \qquad (1.12)$$

R^e is assumed to be homogeneous of degree one in $D + T$ so that we can write

$$R^e = e\,(i, \rho)\,(D + T). \qquad (1.13)$$

The public's rate of supply of assets to the bank, $\mathring{E}^d$, is given by

$$\mathring{E}^d = f\,(i, W, E^d) \qquad (1.14)$$

where W is the public's wealth and E^d the public's desired portfolio of liabilities to the banks. The public's desired rates of change in currency holdings and time deposits are given by

$$\mathring{C}^p = q^1\,(kD - C^p) \qquad (1.15)$$

$$\mathring{T} = q^2\,(tD - T) \qquad (1.16)$$

where k is the desired currency to demand deposit ratio, t is the desired time deposit to demand deposit ratio, and D is the level of demand deposits.

The banks' desired rate of change of indebtedness to the Federal Reserve System is

$$\mathring{A} = a\,[b\,(D + T) - A] \qquad (1.17)$$

where b is the desired indebtedness ratio.

Based on the above, Brunner and Meltzer write:

$$B = A + B^a \qquad (1.18)$$

$$B = R + C \qquad (1.19)$$

$$R = (r + e)\,(D + T) \qquad (1.20)$$

$$C^p = kD \qquad (1.21)$$

$$T = tD \qquad (1.22)$$

$$A = b\,(D + T) \qquad (1.23)$$

$$E = E\,(i, W) \qquad (1.24)$$

where B^A in the adjusted or "relatively exogenous" base and all other symbols have been previously defined. This system of seven equations is then reduced to two through substitution and with the help of the assumption that B^a and W are given exogenously. These equations are:

$$M^2 = m^2 \, B^a \tag{1.25}$$

$$(m^2 - 1) \, B^a = E \, (i, W) \tag{1.26}$$

where m^2, the money multiplier, is given by

$$m^2 = \frac{1 + k + t}{(r + e - b)(1 + t) + k} \, . \tag{1.27}$$

From Equation 1.26, one of the rates of interest, say i^1 (using their notation), can be determined in terms of the rest of the interest rates, ρ, W, B^a, r, and k. Then this solution for i^1 can be substituted into 1.25,[6] giving M^2 as a function of interest rates i^s $(s \neq 1)$, ρ, B^a, r, and W. In other words, the solution to their two equations yields M^2 and one rate of interest, i^1. Equations 1.25 and 1.26 are the expression of the nonlinear hypothesis.

Of the many other works that might be mentioned briefly,[7] we shall concentrate on the models of Ronald L. Teigen (51) and Frank de Leeuw (16).

The Teigen model is based on the proposition that the total level of reserves in the Federal Reserve System, various rules (such as the reserve requirements), and regular behavioral relations (between currency levels and the total money stock, etc.) "determine a maximum attainable money stock at any given time, and that this quantity (M**) can be considered to be the sum of two parts: one part which is considered to be exogenous and is based on reserves supplied by the Federal Reserve System (R^s),[8] and the other based on reserves created by member bank borrowing (B),[9] and therefore considered endogenous" (p. 478). Teigen's goal is to explain the ratio of the observed money stock (M) to the exogenous segment of the total money supply (M*). He asserts that

6. Since all the terms in m^2 are functions of i and/or ρ.
7. See, for example, Grambley and Chase (27), Meigs (40), Modigliani (44), and Goldfeld (25). These and several other studies cited in the bibliography will not be discussed because of their highly specialized nature.
8. This is M*.
9. This is B*.

this ratio is a function of the profitability of bank lending. The important conclusions of the Teigen model are derived from his definitions of the money stock and the public's demand for currency and demand deposits (which he assumes are a constant proportion of the actual money stock).

$$M = \frac{k}{1 - c - h} (R^s - R^e) + \frac{k}{1 - c - h} (B - \frac{1}{k} D_g') \qquad (1.28)$$

where k is the reciprocal of the weighted average reserve ratio, c is the fraction of M held as currency by the public, h is the fraction of M held by the public as demand deposits in nonmember banks, R^e is excess reserves, and D_g' is U.S. government deposits in member banks.

$$M^* = \frac{k}{1 - c - h} (R^s) = k^* R^s \qquad (1.29)$$

and

$$\frac{M}{M^*} = X(r_c, r) \qquad (1.30)$$

where r is a measure of the return on bank loans and r_c is a measure of the cost of bank loans.

$\partial x / \partial r > 0$ indicating that as the return on loans increases, the endogenous portion of M increases relative to M*. $\partial x / \partial r_c < 0$ indicating that as the cost of loans increases, M* becomes a larger proportion of M.

Thus, Teigen breaks the money stock down into endogenous and exogenous portions and attempts to explain the relation between the actual money stock and the exogenous portion in terms of the returns and costs of bank loans. Changes in these factors presumably change the quantity of loans banks are willing to supply and thus result in portfolio readjustment by the banking system, fueling changes in the actual stock of money.

The de Leeuw model is part of the Brookings-SSRC model. His portion of the overall model deals with the financial sector. There are seven markets: bank reserves, currency, demand deposits, time deposits, U.S. securities, "savings and insurance," and private securities. The sectors included are banks, nonbank financial, the Federal Reserve, the Treasury, and the public. This submodel (of the SSRC model) assumes that the value of real variables is known and does not consider the effects of changes in the various rates of interest, or the money stock on the real variables in the model. (Their effects are measured elsewhere in the Brookings model.)

The model itself is composed of nineteen simultaneous equations, four of which are identities (the reserve identity, etc.) and the rest of which express the desired changes in assets in terms of lagged asset holdings, rates of return, and various short-run constraints on asset holding. Solving this system simultaneously, de Leeuw derives the following expression for the money stock (p. 518):

$$S_M = \frac{RES_{NBC}}{\begin{aligned}&\{1 - R_{DD} + 0.84\,[RRR_{DD}]\,[R_{DD} + R_{DD_{GF}}] + \\ &0.82\,[RRR_{DT}]\,[R_{DT}] + [0.011\,RM_{FRB} - \\ &0.010\,RM_{GBS_3} - 0.007]\,[R_{DD} + R_{DT}]\}\end{aligned}} \qquad (1.31)$$

where S_M is the money supply (private demand deposits [DD] and currency); $R_{DD} = DD/S_M$; $R_{DT} = DT/S_M$; $R_{DD_{GF}} = DD_{GF}/S_M$; DT is private time deposits; RES_{NBC} is unborrowed reserves plus currency held by member banks; RRR_{DD} is a weighted average of required reserve ratios against demand deposits; RRR_{DT} is a weighted average of required reserve ratios against time deposits; DD_{GF} is government demand deposits; RM_{FRB} is the discount rate; and RM_{GBS_3} is the average market yield on three-month Treasury bills. Substituting the definitions for R_{DD} and R_{DT} into 1.31 and using the a_i to replace constants, we have

$$S_M = \frac{RES_{NBC}}{\begin{aligned}&\{1 - \frac{DD}{SM} + a_1\,RRR_{DD}\,(\frac{DD + DD_{GF}}{S_M}) + a_2\,RRR_{DT} \\ &(\frac{DT}{S_M}) + [a_3\,RM_{FRB} - a_4\,RM_{GSB_3} - a_5]\,[\frac{DD + DT}{S_M}]\}\end{aligned}} \qquad (1.32)$$

which clearly shows the dependence of the right-hand side of Equation 1.31 on S_M, supposedly given by Equation 1.31. Solving Equation 1.32 for S_M yields

$$S_M = RES_{NBC} + DD - 0.84 [RRR_{DD}] [DD + DD_{GF}] -$$

$$0.82 RRR_{DT} DT - [0.011 RM_{FRB} - 0.010 RM_{FBS_3} -$$

$$0.007] [DD + DT]. \tag{1.33}$$

Equation 1.33, derived from de Leeuw's expression for the money stock, says that the money supply, S_M, is smaller in size than unborrowed reserves plus currency held by the banks plus private demand deposits. This is a nonsense result and throws suspicion on the entire de Leeuw model.

For the month of April 1969, the appropriate figures (taken from the July 1969 Federal Reserve Bulletin) are (in billions of dollars):

Total reserves	27.079
Borrowings	.996
Unborrowed reserves	26.083
Total demand deposits	152.8
Government demand deposits	5.1
Private demand deposits	147.7
Discount rate	5.5 per cent
Yield on three month bills	6.11 per cent
Time deposits	201.6

Plugging these figures into Equation 1.33 and performing the arithmetic, we find that de Leeuw's equation gives a money supply of $150.64 billion. The actual money supply for April 1969 was $196.7 billion. The difference between de Leeuw's prediction and the actual money stock is primarily the $43.9 billion of currency in circulation in April. As can be seen from Equation 1.33, this component of the money supply has been lost in de Leeuw's formulation.

Of the models reviewed here, the de Leeuw model is most similar to the approach taken in this study. The other models tend to be deficient in two respects. First, they are too aggregative in the sense that the economy is broken down into only three sectors—the government, banks, and the public. No distinctions among households, manufacturing firms, and nonbank financial firms are drawn. Second, they all hide the general equilibrium nature of the monetary mechanism. In the first two models reviewed, the behavior functions of the various sectors are not explicitly specified. The Teigen model, while specifying the public's demands for demand deposits and time deposits, does so in terms of the total money stock, and takes the total stock of money as the independent variable in these functions. While such a formulation will probably yield significant empirical results, from a theoretical point of view it seems awkward to visualize the public changing their holdings of demand and time deposits in response to a change in M rather than because of changes in income, prices, and interest rates. Hiding the general equilibrium nature of the problem also precludes description of the effects of changes in the money stock on the real variables of the economy. (This can be done in the SSRC model, but not by the de Leeuw submodel itself.)

The purpose of this work is, however, not to repudiate any of the existing work in this area, but rather to extend and amplify the analysis begun by these more narrow and specialized studies.

2. The Model

THE MODEL is made up of five sectors: public, manufacturing (the firms), banking (the banks), nonbank financial (the intermediaries), and government. This chapter contains details of each sector and the relationships among sectors. The solution to the model will be considered in chapters 3 and 4.

The behavioral relations for each sector are given in both implicit and explicit form. For simplicity two assumptions are made: most of the explicit forms are linear and reflect either utility or profit maximizing behavior, and the individual units in each sector are homogeneous so that, in most cases, aggregate levels can be obtained by summing the representative functions.

PRODUCTION, INVESTMENT, AND GROWTH

Technology is assumed to be characterized by increasing opportunity costs and is constant over time. For simplicity these assumptions are made:

1. There are only two inputs—capital and labor. A unit of labor is indistinguishable from any other unit of labor. Capital is also perfectly homogeneous.

2. There are only two outputs—capital and the consumption good. The consumption good is perfectly homogeneous.

3. Firms fall into two categories—those that produce only the capital good and those that produce only the consumer good. Each firm within each category is identical to every other firm in the group. There is a large enough number of firms in each category so that, coupled with freedom of entry and exit, each firm is a perfect competitor in the output market.

4. Individuals in the economy have identical endowments of capital and labor. No organization controls the supply of either capital or labor.

Thus, the capital good firms are also perfect competitors in the input market and the labor market is perfectly competitive.

Production

The aggregate production function for the capital good is given by

$$X_k^a = X_k (L_k, X_{kk}) \tag{2.1}$$

where L_k is the amount of labor used in the production of capital and X_{kk} is the amount of capital used in the production of capital,

$$\frac{\partial X_k^a}{\partial L_k} > 0, \quad \frac{\partial X_k^a}{\partial X_{kk}} > 0, \quad \frac{\partial^2 X_k^a}{\partial L_k^2} < 0, \quad \frac{\partial^2 X_k^a}{\partial X_{kk}^2} < 0,$$

and

$$\frac{\partial^2 X_k^a}{\partial L_k \, \partial X_{kk}} \gtreqless 0.$$

If there are n firms producing capital, the production function for the ith individual firm is

$$X_{ki} = \frac{X_k^a}{n} = X_k \left(\frac{L_k}{n}, \frac{X_{kk}}{n}\right). \tag{2.2}$$

The aggregate production function for the consumer good firms is given by

$$X_c^a = X_c(L_c, X_{kc}) \tag{2.3}$$

where L_c is the amount of labor used in the production of the consumption good and X_{kc} is the amount of capital used in the production of the consumption good.

$$\frac{\partial^2 X_c^a}{\partial L_c} > 0, \quad \frac{\partial X_c^a}{\partial X_{kc}} > 0, \quad \frac{\partial^2 X_c^a}{\partial L_c^2} < 0, \quad \frac{\partial^2 X_c^a}{\partial X_{kc}^2} < 0,$$

and

$$\frac{\partial^2 X_c^a}{\partial X_{kc} \, \partial L_c} \gtrless 0.$$

If there are m firms producing the consumer good, the production function for the jth firm is

$$X_{cj} = \frac{X_c^a}{m} = X_c \left(\frac{L_c}{m}, \frac{X_{kc}}{m} \right). \tag{2.4}$$

The transformation curve is shown in Figure 1. The transformation function is given by

$$X_c = T(X_k) \tag{2.5}$$

where

1. $T(0) = \alpha_{ci}$

2. $T(\alpha_{ki}) = 0$

3. $\dfrac{\partial X_k}{\partial X_c} < 0.$

α_{ci} is the maximum production of the consumption good in period i while α_{ki} represents the maximum production of capital for the same period. Defining the transformation function implicitly we have

$$T'(X_k, X_c) = 0. \tag{2.6}$$

Thus $\bar{X} = (\bar{X}_k, \bar{X}_c)$ is a full-employment output vector if

$$T'(\bar{X}_k, \bar{X}_c) = 0. \tag{2.7}$$

$\bar{X}' = (X'_k, X'_c)$ is less than full employment if

$$T'(X'_k, X'_c) < 0. \tag{2.8}$$

If $T' < 0$ the unused productive potential of the economy is measured by the negative value of T. The economy is in full-employment equilibrium if 2.6 is satisfied and if $P_c/P_k = dX_k/dX_c$. For purposes of the model it is assumed that the explicit form of 2.5 is

$$X_{ci}^2 + X_{ki}^2 = \alpha_{ki}^2 \tag{2.9}$$

and $\alpha_{ci} = \alpha_{ki}$ for all i. Thus the explicit transformation curve assumed is a quarter circle in the positive quadrant. Writing 2.9 in a form equiva-

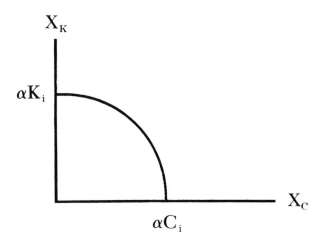

Fig. 1. The transformation curve

lent to 2.2 we have that $X_i' = (X_{ci}', X_{ki}')$ is a full-employment output vector if

$$X_{ki}' = \sqrt{\alpha_{ki}^2 - X_{ci}'^2}, X_{ki}' \geq 0. \tag{2.10}$$

The marginal rate of transformation is

$$\text{MRT} = -\frac{dX_c}{dX_k} = +\frac{X_k}{(\alpha_k^2 - X_k^2)^{1/2}}. \tag{2.11}$$

When 2.10 is satisfied, output is at full employment and where, in addition, 2.11 is equal to the price ratio, output is also an equilibrium output.

The explicit form of 2.7 is simply

$$X_{ci}^2 + X_{ki}^2 - \alpha_{ki}^2 = 0. \tag{2.12}$$

Growth and Investment

The labor force is assumed to grow at the same rate as the population. This rate is assumed to be a function of the rate of change of the real output of the consumption good over time.

$$\frac{dL}{dt} / L = \lambda = \lambda \left(\frac{dX_c}{dt} \right) \tag{2.13}$$

where λ is the rate of growth of the labor force, $\lambda(dX_c/dt)$ is functional notation, and where

$$1 \geq \frac{d\lambda}{d(\frac{dX_c}{dt})} > 0.$$

The rate of growth of the capital stock, k, is not tied to the rate of growth of the labor force. Gross and net investment are determined by the interaction of the supply and demand for capital. In general, however, k is assumed to be a function of the price of capital, the price of the firms' output, the firms' profit expectations, the various rates of interest, the rate of depreciation, and the existing stock of capital. The demand for capital is composed of both a stock demand for capital, D_k, and a flow demand, dK.[1] The stock demand is given by

$$D_k = D_k(P_k, r, \emptyset) \tag{2.14}$$

where r is a vector of interest rates ($r = (r_f, r_g, r_t, \text{etc.})$) and $\emptyset$ is a profit expectation function; also

$$\frac{\partial D_k}{\partial P_k} < 0, \quad \frac{\partial D_k}{\partial r} < 0, \quad \text{and} \quad \frac{\partial D_K}{\partial \emptyset} > 0.$$

The flow demand for capital, dK, is given by

$$dK = nK \tag{2.15}$$

where n is the rate of depreciation, $0 < n < 1$, and K is the existing capital stock.

1. See P. Davidson (13).

The supply of capital is also composed of a stock supply and a flow supply. The stock supply, S_k, is simply equal to the existing capital stock, while the flow supply, s_k, is assumed to be dependent on the price of capital.

$$s_k = s_k(P_k) \tag{2.16}$$

where

$$\frac{ds_k}{dP_k} > 0.$$

In Figure 2, $D_k + dK$ is the market (stock + flow) demand for capital and $S_k + s_k$ is the market (stock + flow) supply of capital. $\bar{P}_k$ is the

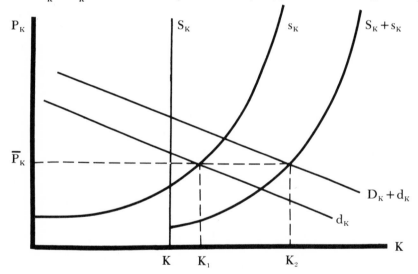

Fig. 2. Supply and demand for capital

equilibrium price of capital. At this price gross investment is equal to $K_2 - K$ and net investment equal to $K_1 - K$.

Note that it is the rates of interest relevant for financing and determining relevant discount rates that, along with profit expectations, determine the exact locations of D_k. As rates fall, D_k shifts outward, ceteris paribus.

Although it would be more elegant to consider gross and net investment for each group of firms separately, we shall assume that 2.14–16 are defined in such a manner that their solution as shown in Figure 2 represents the aggregate levels of gross and net investment for both groups of firms combined.

The rate of growth of the capital stock, k, is, in terms of Figure 2,

$$k = \frac{K + K_1 - K}{K} = \frac{K_1}{K}. \tag{2.17}$$

We must now consider the effects of changes in the capital stock and the labor force on the transformation curve, given that technology is constant. The question is basically this: if L_t, K_t give $\alpha_{kt} = \alpha_{ct}$, what will α_{ct+1} and α_{kt+1} equal if L grows by λ_t per cent and K grows by k_t per cent, $\lambda_t >/< k_t$, e.g., what relation will the transformation curve in t + 1 bear to the curve in t? Will relation 2.9 hold over time? If not, what other assumptions about the nature of production must we make to insure that it does?

Writing the total differentials of the production functions, we have

$$dX_c = \frac{\partial X_c}{\partial K_c} dK_c + \frac{\partial X_c}{\partial L_c} dL_c \tag{2.18}$$

$$dX_k = \frac{\partial X_k}{\partial K_k} dK_k + \frac{\partial X_k}{\partial L_k} dL_k. \tag{2.19}$$

From the definitions of k and λ,

$$k = \frac{\dot{K}}{K} = \frac{dK}{dt} / K \tag{2.20}$$

$$\lambda = \frac{\dot{L}}{L} = \frac{dL}{dt} / L, \tag{2.21}$$

we have

$$\frac{dK}{dt} = kK \tag{2.22}$$

and

$$\frac{dL}{dt} = \lambda L, \tag{2.23}$$

from which it follows that

$$dK = kKdt \tag{2.24}$$

and

$$dL = \lambda Ldt. \tag{2.25}$$

Substituting 2.24 and 2.25 into 2.18 and 2.19 we have

$$dX_c = \frac{\partial X_c}{\partial K} kKdt + \frac{\partial X_c}{\partial L} \lambda Ldt \tag{2.26}$$

and

$$dX_k = \frac{\partial X_k}{\partial K} kKdt + \frac{\partial X_k}{\partial L} \lambda Ldt \tag{2.27}$$

from which it follows that

$$\frac{dX_c}{dt} = \frac{\partial X_c}{\partial X} kK + \frac{\partial X_c}{\partial L} \lambda L \tag{2.28}$$

and

$$\frac{\partial X_k}{\partial t} = \frac{\partial X_k}{\partial K} kK + \frac{X_k}{L} \lambda L. \tag{2.29}$$

Equations 2.28 and 2.29 tell us how the maximum possible outputs of the consumer good and the capital good change over time if the entire increase in the stocks of labor and capital is used in one good or the other. In order for the transformation curve to shift in a parallel way as a result of the growth of capital and labor, it is necessary and sufficient that 2.28 equal 2.29. Since we are starting from a position where $\alpha_c = \alpha_k$, only the rates of change need be equal to insure the increase in α_c is equal to the increase in α_k. Thus we have

$$\frac{\partial X_c}{\partial K_c} \, kK + \frac{\partial X_c}{\partial L_c} \, \lambda L = \frac{\partial X_k}{\partial K_k} \, kK + \frac{\partial X_k}{\partial L_k} \, \lambda L. \tag{2.30}$$

Equation 2.30 can be rewritten in two ways, both of which express the condition necessary for a parallel shift of the transformation curve.

$$(1) \quad kK \left(\frac{\partial X_c}{\partial K_c} - \frac{\partial X_k}{\partial K_k} \right) + \lambda L \left(\frac{\partial X_c}{\partial L_c} - \frac{\partial X_k}{\partial L_k} \right) = 0$$

Regardless of the relative sizes of k and λ and of their signs, if the marginal product of capital in production of the consumer good is equal to its marginal product in producing capital, and if the same is true of the marginal products of labor in its two uses, (1) will be satisfied. If these marginal products are not equal, (2) expresses the condition that must be satisfied for parallel shifts. Number (2) is also derived directly from 2.30.

$$(2) \quad \frac{\lambda L}{kK} = \frac{\dfrac{\partial X_k}{\partial K_k} - \dfrac{\partial X_c}{\partial K_c}}{\dfrac{\partial X_c}{\partial L_c} - \dfrac{\partial X_k}{\partial L_k}}$$

Since (2) places no unrealistic constraints on the production processes, we assume that it is satisfied for all λ and k between ± 1.

The Labor Market

The aggregate supply of labor is a function of the wage rate, P_ℓ, and the size of the population. If it is assumed that the labor force is a constant percentage of the population, we may write

$$S^\ell = S^\ell(P_\ell, L) \tag{2.31}$$

where

$$\frac{\partial S^\ell}{\partial P_\ell} > 0 \text{ and } \frac{\partial S^\ell}{\partial L} > 0.$$

At any point in time, the supply of labor may be taken to be a function of only the price of labor.

The aggregate demand for labor is composed of the demand of the capital good firms and the consumer good firms, as well as the demands of the banks, government, and intermediaries. No attempt will be made to specify explicitly the demand functions for these sectors. (This is in keeping with the practice of not specifying these sectors' demand for the capital good explicitly.) This demand is included by adding a constant, E, to the sum of 2.32 and 2.33. These demands are

$$D_k^{\ell} = MP_{\ell k}P_k \tag{2.32}$$

$$D_c^{\ell} = MP_{\ell c}P_c \tag{2.33}$$

since all firms are perfect competitors.

The aggregate demand is simply

$$D^{\ell} = MP_{\ell k}P_k + MP_{\ell c}PX_c + E. \tag{2.34}$$

Under our assumptions on production, the aggregate demand curve will be downward sloping. Since labor is homogeneous, it must be paid the same wage in each use. Thus we have Figure 3. $\bar{P}_{\ell}$ is the equilibrium

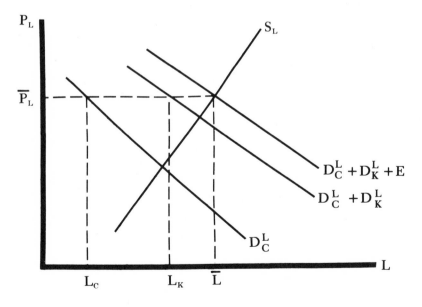

Fig. 3. Supply and demand for labor

price of labor. The amounts employed by each group of firms can be read from the diagram: $\bar{L}$ is the total amount employed, L_c the amount used by the consumer good firms, and $\bar{L} - L_c$ the amount employed by the capital good firms. No restrictions are placed on $d\bar{P}_c/dt$, e.g., no assumption of wage inflexibility is made. Thus, in one sense, labor will be fully employed so long as the existing P_ℓ is an equilibrium price. If $P_c > \bar{P}_\ell$, involuntary unemployment exists. If $P_\ell < \bar{P}_\ell$, labor is fully employed, even though there is a positive excess demand for labor.

Production Equilibrium and Full Employment

These conditions must be satisfied for the productive sector of the economy to be in equilibrium:

1. P_ℓ is equal in both uses.

2. P_k is equal in both uses.

3. $P_\ell = MP_{\ell k}P_k = MP_{\ell c}P_c$.

4. $P_k = MP_{k k}P_k = MP_{k c}P_c$.

Condition 4 clearly implies that the marginal product of capital in the production of capital must be 1 in equilibrium. This is not startling, since the capital good firms would obviously increase their own use of capital if $MP_{k k} > 1$ and reduce it if $MP_{k k} < 1$.

5. The marginal rate of technical substitution of labor for capital equals the input price ratio for both groups of firms.

$$\text{a. } MRTS^k_{k/\ell} = \frac{MP_{k k}}{MP_{\ell k}} = \frac{P_k}{P_\ell} .$$

$$\text{b. } MRTS^c_{k/\ell} = \frac{MP_{k c}}{MP_{\ell c}} = \frac{P_k}{P_\ell} .$$

6. $MRTS^k_{k/\ell} = MRTS^c_{k/\ell} = \dfrac{P_k}{P_\ell} .$

When conditions 1–6 are satisfied, the productive sector is in equilibrium in the sense that, given the total amounts of the inputs being used, it is impossible to increase output of the earlier commodity by redistributing the capital and labor being used between the two groups of firms without reducing the output of the other commodity. However, 1–6 are not sufficient to insure that the equilibrium output vector is also a full-employment output vector. This is simply because nothing in these conditions implies that the total stocks of capital and labor are being used. That is, 1–6 may be satisfied under conditions of unemployed labor and/or capital. In this case, even though redistribution of the inputs actually being used cannot increase the output of one commodity without reducing the output of the other, it is entirely possible that increasing the total use of capital and/or labor can lead to an increase in the production of both goods. Thus, another condition must be added to insure that the equilibrium is also a full-employment equilibrium. This condition is simply that the outputs of capital and the consumer goods that satisfy 1–6 also satisfy

$$7. \quad \bar{X}_k \; = \; \sqrt{\alpha_k^2 - \bar{X}_c^2} \, ,$$

where $\bar{X}_k$ and $\bar{X}_c$ are the outputs resulting from satisfying 1–6. Note that the aggregate level of consumption demand, not yet considered, has an impact on these conditions through its influence on P_c and $\bar{X}_c$ and, of course, may prevent condition 7 from being satisfied.

The Manufacturing Sector (Firms)

The firms are divided into two groups: one produces only the capital good while the other produces only the consumer good. Each group is assumed to be perfectly competitive. The only interfirm purchases are those of capital goods. Each group will be treated in the aggregate rather than on an individual firm basis.

Production and sales for each firm in a group are identical (see the section on production in this chapter). Each firm has a desired level of retained earnings such that the aggregate desired level is given by

$$E_t^D = \alpha K_t + \beta I_{nt-1} + s[P_{ct} \, X_{ct} + P_{kt} \, X_{kt}]. \tag{2.35}$$

In 2.1, αK_t represents depreciation; $P_{ct} \, X_{ct} + P_{kt} \, X_{kt}$ is, of course, aggregate sales in t; and s is a constant, $0 < s < 1$. This term is included to reflect the demand for retained earnings arising from the desire of the firm to insure itself from the unexpected. Such risks are simplistically assumed to grow in proportion to total sales. βI_{nt-1} is a factor reflecting the influence of past net investment on the level of retained earnings, a portion of which, it is assumed, are kept to meet the demand for financing net investment in future periods. For simplicity only one previous net investment figure is used in 2.35, although greater realism could be obtained by perhaps using averages of several past periods. It is assumed that β is greater than zero and less than one. Equation 2.35 also gives the desired level of financial assets—cash, demand deposits, time deposits, government securities, and deposits in intermediaries—in the aggregate for period t, since it is in these forms that retained earnings are held. At the end of each period the actual and desired stocks of retained earnings are equalized by adjustment of the profit payments to the owners of the firms. Only when profit payments are zero would it be possible for the actual stock of retained earnings to be less than the desired level. In no case will the actual stock exceed the desired level.

Before discussing the desired distribution of the stock of retained earnings, another factor influencing the actual stock must be discussed. This is the relationship between desired financing and actual financing. The replacement demand for capital, $I_g - I_n$, is assumed to be paid for completely out of retained earnings. Only a portion of net investment, equal to βI_{nt-1}, is paid for from retained earnings. The remainder, $I_{nt} - \beta I_{nt-1}$, creates the so-called demand for financing. This demand is the basis for the firms' demand for bank loans and loans from intermediaries and for their desire to issue more debt (the supply of firms' nonownership securities). We have

$$F_t^D = I_{nt} - \beta I_{nt-1} \tag{2.36}$$

where F_t^D is the desired level of financing in period t.

$$L_{ft}^D = f_2(r, F_t^D) \tag{2.37}$$

explicitly,

$$L_{ft}^D = \ell_f F_t^D + A_3 \overline{r}_f \tag{2.38}$$

where L_{ft}^D is firms' total demand for loans in t, A_3 is a vector of constants, $\overline{r}_f$ is a vector of all interest rates, and F_t^D the total amount of financing desired.

$$F_t^S = f_3(\bar{r}_f, F_t^D)$$ (2.39)

explicitly,

$$F_t^S = b_f F_t^D + A_4 \bar{r}_f$$ (2.40)

where F_t^S is the supply of firms' securities in t and all other symbols are as defined above. The firms' demand for loans, L_{ft}^D, is broken down into a demand for bank loans, L_{ft}^{Db}, and a demand for loans from intermediaries, L_{ft}^{Dn},

$$L_{ft}^{Db} = L_f^{Db} (r_{bt}^f, r_{nt}^f, L_{ft}^D)$$ (2.41)

$$L_{ft}^{Dn} = L_f^{Dn} (r_{bft}^f, r_{nft}, L_{ft}^D).$$ (2.42)

In explicit form,

$$L_{ft}^{Db} = a_1(r_{bt}^f - r_{nt}^f) + b_1 L_{ft}^D$$ (2.43)

$$L_{ft}^{Dn} = a_2(r_{bt}^f - r_{nt}^f) + b_2 L_{ft}^D$$ (2.44)

where $a_1 = -a_2$, $b_1 + b_2 = 1$, $a_1 < 0$, $a_2 > 0$. These restrictions on the constants in 2.43 and 2.44 insure that the sum of 2.43 and 2.44 equals 2.37. The coefficients of L_{ft}^D are assumed to be constant (and not necessarily equal) to allow for the possibility that the firms may want to borrow different amounts from the two lending sectors even though $r_b^f = r_n^f$. This mix of desired borrowing is assumed to be constant over time. If L_{ft} is the net increase in borrowing and F_t the net increase in securities outstanding, then

$$I_{nt} - \beta I_{nt-1} - (L_{ft} + B_{ft}) \geq 0.$$ (2.45)

L_{ft} and F_t are determined by the interaction of the demand for loans (the supply of securities) and the supply of loans to firms (the total demand for firms' securities). If 2.41 equals zero, then the financing demand is satisfied completely by increasing the firms' debt. If, however, 2.41 is positive, the difference is made up by a temporary reduction in the stock of retained earnings below their desired level. (Note that the capital good firms do not themselves extend credit to their

purchasers.) This discrepancy between desired and actual retained earnings is made up by a reduction in profit payments as discussed before.
Let

$$I_{nt} - \beta I_{nt-1} - (L_{ft} + B_{ft}) = \Delta I(A_{ft}) > 0 \tag{2.46}$$

where $\Delta I(A_{ft})$ represents the unintended change in the firms' financial asset position caused by insufficient financing to meet investment demand. $\Delta I(A_{ft})$ represents a redistribution of income away from the owners of the consumer good firms to the owners of capital good firms. As we shall see, aggregate public income is not reduced. In summary,

$$E_t^D \equiv E_{t+}^a = E_{t-}^a + \Delta E_t^D \tag{2.47}$$

where E_{t+}^a is the actual stock of retained earnings (or, equivalently, the actual stock of financial assets, A_{ft+}^a) at the end of period t; E_{t-}^a is the actual stock of retained earnings at the beginning of period t, which is equal to the actual and desired stock of retained earnings at the end of period $t - 1$; and ΔE_t^D is the desired change in the stock of retained earnings during t.

ΔE_t^D can be expressed as follows:

$$\Delta E_t^D = \alpha I_{nt-1} + s[P_{ct} X_{ct} + P_{kt} X_{kt} - P_{ct-1} X_{ct-1} -$$

$$P_{kt-1} X_{kt-1}] + \beta(I_{nt-1} - I_{nt-2}). \tag{2.48}$$

Furthermore, $P_{ct} X_{ct} + P_{kt} X_{kt}$ can be written as a function of K_t:

$$P_{ct} X_{ct} + P_{kt} X_{kt} = f_3(K_t). \tag{2.49}$$

The function f_3 is really a reduced form of the production function. The level of output is determinate, given the amount of capital used under the assumption that, for a particular input price ratio, the least-cost combination of labor and capital is used. Thus, 2.44 becomes

$$\Delta E_t^D = \alpha I_{nt-1} + s[f_3(K_t) - f_3(K_{t-1})] +$$

$$\beta(I_{nt-1} - I_{nt-2}) \tag{2.50}$$

or

$$= \alpha I_{nt-1} + s[f_3(K_{t-1} + I_{nt-1}) - f_3(K_{t-2} +$$
$$I_{nt-2})] + \beta(I_{nt-1} - I_{nt-2}) \qquad (2.51)$$

or

$$= \alpha I_{nt-1} + s[f_3(K_{t-1} + I_{nt-1}) - f(K_{t-2} +$$
$$I_{nt-2})] + \beta(I_{nt-1} - I_{nt-2}) \qquad (2.52)$$

or

$$= \alpha I_{nt-1} + s[f_3(K_{t-1} - K_{t-2} + I_{nt-1} - I_{nt-2})]$$
$$+ \beta(I_{nt-1} - I_{nt-2}) \qquad (2.53)$$

or

$$= \alpha I_{nt-1} + s[f_3(I_{nt-1})] + \beta(I_{nt-1} - I_{nt-1}). \qquad (2.54)$$

Letting $(\alpha + \beta)(I_{nt-1}) + sf_3(I_{nt-1})$ equal $f_4(I_{nt-1})$ we have

$$\Delta E_t^D = f_4(I_{nt-1}) - \beta(I_{nt-2}) \qquad (2.55)$$

which expresses the dependency of desired changes in retained earnings on net investment. Summing over t in 2.55 (or integrating when time is assumed to be continuous) leads to the dependency of the stock of retained earnings on the capital stock as expressed in 2.35. Rewriting 2.35 in an analogous manner leads to

$$E_t^D = \alpha K_t + sf_3(K_t) + \beta(K_t - K_{t-1}) \qquad (2.56)$$

or

$$= (\alpha + \beta) K_t + sf_3(K_t) - \beta(K_{t-1})$$

or, letting $(\alpha + \beta) K_t + sf_3(K_t) = f_3(K_t)$,

$$E_t^D = f_3(K_t) - \beta(K_{t-1}). \qquad (2.57)$$

The firms' decision-making process in regard to the size and distribution of retained earnings is visualized in this manner. First a decision is made regarding the desired stock of retained earnings and the necessary adjustments of profit payments made to realize this goal. Second, after desired size has been achieved, the firm decides on the desired distribution of retained earnings (financial assets) as described below. Letting DE_t^D represent the desired distribution of retained earnings in t, we have:

$$DE_t^D \equiv DA_{ft}^D = f_4(r, PX) \tag{2.58}$$

where DA_{ft}^D is the desired distribution of financial assets, r is a vector of all interest rates, and $PX = P_c X_c + P_k X_k$. DA_{ft}^D is itself a vector, the elements of which are cash balances, demand deposits, time deposits, government securities, and deposits in intermediaries. Firms are assumed to hold no debt instruments issued by other firms. Thus,

$$DA_{ft}^D = (C_{ft}^D, D_{ft}^D, T_{ft}^D, G_{ft}^D, N_{ft}^D). \tag{2.59}$$

Obviously,

$$\sum_{i=1}^{5} (DA_{ft}^D)_i \equiv A_{ft}^D. \tag{2.60}$$

Equation 2.53 can be broken down into an interdependent system of equations each giving the desired level of one asset. The desired level of cash balances, C_{ft}^D, is assumed to depend only on the level of sales. Thus,

$$C_{ft}^D = a_5 [P_{ct} X_{ct} + P_{kt} X_{kt}] \tag{2.61}$$

where a_5 is a constant, $0 < a_5 < 1$. Changes in rates of interest are assumed not to affect desired currency balances, although they are assumed to influence the desired level of demand deposits. Equation 2.61 is designed to reflect the assumption that holding currency balances is a nuisance to the firms and such balances are held to an absolute minimum. The desired level of demand deposits is assumed to be a function of the level of sales, the rate of interest on time deposits, and the rate of interest on government securities. Thus,

$$D_{ft}^D = d_f(PX) + A_6 \bar{r}_f. \tag{2.62}$$

The desired levels of time deposits and government securities are also functions of the same variables. Thus,

$$T_{ft}^D = t_f(PX) + A_7 \bar{r}_f; \tag{2.63}$$

$$G_{ft}^D = g_f(PX) + A_8 \bar{r}_f; \tag{2.64}$$

$$N_{ft}^D = n_f(PX) + A_9 \bar{r}_f. \tag{2.65}$$

We now turn to an examination of the sources and uses of income for the firms in the consumer good group. There are four sources of income for these firms: sales, interest on time deposits, interest on government securities, and interest on deposits in intermediaries. Let R_{ft} be the receipts (income) of these firms in period t. Then

$$R_{f_{ct}} = PX_t + r_{g_t} G_{t_{ct}} + r_{t_t} T_{f_{ct}} + r_{n_t} N_{f_{ct}}. \tag{2.66}$$

The uses of income include these six: payments to labor, profit payments ("dividends"), changes in financial asset holdings, loan repayments, debt (security) retirement, and investment expenditure. The first two are treated strictly as residuals and are represented by Y_{f_c} (income received by the public from consumer good firms). Changes in financial asset holdings are equal to ΔE_{ct}^D. Loan repayments equal

$$\sum_{i=t-n}^{t} \left[\frac{(1 + r_{bf}(i))L_f^b(i)}{N} \right] + \sum_{i=t-n}^{t} \left[\frac{(1 + r_{nf}(i))L_f^n(i)}{N} \right]$$

abbreviated ΣL_f. Debt retirement equals

$$\sum_{i=t-n}^{t} \left[\frac{(1 + r_{fc}(i))F_c(i)}{N} \right]$$

abbreviated ΣF_c. Gross investment equals I_{g_c}. Let U_{f_c} represent the sum of one through five. Then

$$U_{g_{ct}} = Y_{f_{ct}} + \Delta A_{f_{ct}} + \Sigma L_{f_c} + \Sigma F_c. \tag{2.67}$$

However, $R_{f_{ct}} < U_{f_{ct}}$ since part of net investment must be financed. Let S_{f_c} be total spending power of the consumer good firms in t. Then

$$S_{f_{ct}} = R_{f_{ct}} + L_{f_{ct}} + F_{ct} \tag{2.68}$$

and

$$S_{f_{ct}} = U_{f_{ct}}. \tag{2.69}$$

Inclusion of the capital good firms allows the elimination of the c subscript in 2.65 to 2.68. It is assumed a typical capital good firm, even though it satisfies its demand for capital goods from its own output, has a financing demand identical to the consumer good firm, and behaves otherwise in the manner described above. Thus, aggregation over all firms yields the detailed statement of 2.69:

$$PX_t + r_{g_t} G_{ft} + r_{t_t} T_{ft} + r_{n_t} N_{ft} + L_{ft} + B_{ft} =$$

$$\Delta(A_{ft}) + \Sigma L_{ft} + \Sigma B_{ft} + P_{kt} X_{kft} + Y_{ft} \tag{2.70}$$

$$Y_{ft} = PX_t + r_{g_t} G_{ft} + r_{t_t} T_{ft} + r_{n_t} N_{ft} + L_{ft} +$$

$$B_{ft} - \Delta(A_{ft}) - \Sigma L_{ft} - \Sigma F_{ft} - P_{kt} X_{kft}. \tag{2.71}$$

The Government Sector

All levels of government are treated together—that is, as if there were only one government. No attempt is made to reflect the actual institutional constraints under which "government" operates. There are two functions our government performs.

1. *Reallocation*—All physical production is assumed to take place in the manufacturing sector. The government buys capital and the consumption good from the firms. A portion of these goods is consumed by the government and a portion is distributed to the public free of charge.

2. *Economic regulation*—Fiscal policy is not consciously used to regulate the level of economic activity. Government spending is limited to the acquisition of the amount of goods necessary for the operation of the government and for making the (exogenously determined) transfer payments. Tax receipts are assumed to be equal to these expenditures plus the interest payments on government securities. Conscious economic regulation is attempted through monetary policy exclusively. The

standard monetary tools are available open-market operations, changes in the discount rate, and changes in reserve requirements, each of which will be considered in detail in chapter 4.

Taxes and Government Spending

All taxes are assumed to be paid by the individuals in the economy. No taxes are explicitly levied on the banks, firms, or intermediaries. All profits over and above the requirements for retained earnings to meet future investment are paid to the individual owners of these enterprises. This income is taxed at the same rate as income received from other sources (wage and interest payments). We have then

$$T = t\overline{Y} \qquad (2.72)$$

where T is total tax receipts, t the tax rate, and $\overline{Y}$ aggregate public income before taxes. It is assumed that t is constant to reflect an earlier assumption of no conscious fiscal policy. Furthermore, government spending is given by

$$T = \overline{r}_g\overline{G} + P_kX_{kg} + P_cX_{cg} \qquad (2.73)$$

where $\overline{r}_g$ and $\overline{G}$ represent the coupon rate and aggregate face value of government securities outstanding, respectively (see the next section). The amounts of capital and the consumer good purchased are determined residually:

$$P_kX_{kg} = \theta\,(T - \overline{r}_g\overline{G}) \qquad (2.74)$$

$$P_cX_{cg} = (1 - \theta)\,(T - \overline{r}_g\overline{G}) \qquad (2.75)$$

where θ is a positive constant less than 1. These relations insure that the budget is balanced.

Government Securities and Monetary Affairs

The government issues only one type of security with one-year maturity and fixed face value of $1. The coupon rate is fixed at $\overline{r}_g$. The actual rate in any period, r_g, may, of course, differ from the coupon rate depending on whether or not the bond is sold at its face value. If P_g is the price of one security, then

$$\bar{r}_g = P_g r_g \tag{2.76}$$

or

$$r_g = \frac{\bar{r}_g}{P_g}. \tag{2.77}$$

At the end of each year the holder of a bond receives $\$(1 + \bar{r}_g)$ payment of interest and principal. The government is not required to buy back unmatured bonds, although they may be freely traded among individuals and corporate entities. The amounts and timing of government sales and purchases of government securities may be determined either by purely passive reaction to the net demand of the nongovernment sectors or may be determined by conscious monetary policy goals. This area will be examined in detail in chapters 3 and 4.

In any event, the effect of net changes in the amount of government securities outstanding will be to change the stock of money in the hands of the private sectors. Suppose $P_{gt}G_t$ dollars in bonds were issued at the beginning of period t. At the end of the period $(1 + \bar{r}_g)G_t$ dollars are paid out in interest and principal. In $t + 1$, $P_{gt + 1}G_{t + 1}$ dollars worth of bonds are issued and interest and principal payments are $(1 + \bar{r}_g)G_{t + 1}$ at the end of the period. The initial impact on the money stock in period $t + 1$ is given by $(1 + \bar{r}_g)G_t - P_{gt + 1}G_{t + 1}$. If this is positive, the refunding increases the money stock by $(1 + \bar{r}_g)G_t - P_{gt + 1}G_{t + 1}$ times the appropriate multiplier; if negative, the money stock is decreased. The effect of refunding in $t + 2$ will be given by $(1 + \bar{r}_g)G_{t + 1} - P_{gt + 2}G_{t + 2}$ times the appropriate multiplier, etc. The government's ability to control G, the number of bonds issued, and P_g (or r_g) is the key element in open-market operations. The size of the multiplier and the strength of the relations between the stock of money and real variables determine the effectiveness of this sort of monetary policy (see chapter 4).

When solving the model in the absence of discretionary monetary policy, we shall assume that the government's supply of bonds is infinitely elastic at the current rate of interest (price of bonds). In chapter 4, this assumption will be removed. Thus,

$$G^S \equiv G^{Da} \tag{2.78}$$

where G^S is the supply of bonds and G^{Da} the aggregate demand for new bonds. This implies that the price of bonds (actual rate of interest on government securities) is constant over time.

The rediscount mechanism is assumed to operate in the following manner. All loans made by the banks are discounts and are assumed to be eligible paper. The rediscount rate, r_d, is a percentage of the face value of the notes held by the bank. The bank receives $(1 - r_d)X$ when it rediscounts a note whose face is X dollars. If the total value of the bank's loan portfolio in any period is Y dollars, the maximum amount of rediscounting is $(1 - r_d)Y$.

The government is assumed to rediscount as much paper as the banks offer at the current rediscount rate. The rate itself is set by the monetary authority (see chapter 4). Thus, for any rediscount rate,

$$d \equiv d^d(r_d) \tag{2.79}$$

where d is the actual amount of rediscounting and d^d the quantity of rediscounting demanded at rate r_d.

The effect of rediscounting is, as will be shown, to increase the quantity of bank loans supplied.

The government (monetary authority) also establishes, and is free to charge, the reserve requirement, r. It is assumed that both time and demand deposits are subject to the same reserve requirements. Thus, the total amount of required reserves, R, is given by

$$R = r (D + T) \tag{2.80}$$

where D is the aggregate level of demand deposits and T the aggregate level of time deposits. All banks in the economy are assumed to be subject to the regulation of the monetary authority. Effects of change in the reserve requirement on the stock of money are discussed in chapter 4.

The government is strictly a passive supplier-absorber of currency. Thus, at any point in time, the stock of currency, C_t, is identical to the aggregate demand for currency, C_t^{Da}. Thus,

$$C_t \equiv C_t^{Da}. \tag{2.81}$$

Until monetary policy is considered explicitly, the government is essentially passive in the model.

THE BANKING SECTOR

Banks perform two major functions: they accept time and demand deposits from the public, the firms, and the intermediaries, and they make loans to the public and the firms. As adjuncts to these services they also hold currency and government securities as secondary reserves, engage in rediscounting, and hold primary reserves.

Time and Demand Deposits

Time deposits earn a yearly rate of interest, r_t. This rate is paid on all time deposits regardless of their source (public, firm, or intermediary). The banks view all time deposits as homogeneous, regardless of their source. Even though some time deposits (or demand deposits) may be held as compensatory balances, no attempt is made to distinguish this portion of deposits from "ordinary" time or demand deposits. The banks' demand for time deposits is perfectly elastic at the current rate of interest on time deposits. Banks "buy" the total of time deposits willing to be "sold" by the other sectors at the prevailing rate on time deposits. Thus, letting T^D represent the banks' demand for time deposits, we have

$$T^D \equiv T_p^S + T_f^S + T_n^S \tag{2.82}$$

where T_p^S, T_f^S, and T_n^S represent the quantity of time deposits by the three sectors. T_t is the total level of time deposits in period t; thus,

$$T_t = T_t^D \equiv T_{pt}^S + T_{ft}^S + T_{nt}^S. \tag{2.83}$$

The rate banks pay on time deposits is assumed to depend on the profitability of loans and the cost of obtaining reserves from alternate sources. The rates of loans to the public (r_{bp}) and to the firms (r_{bf}) minus the rate on time deposits are surrogates for profitability. The only other source of reserves under the control of the banks is the rediscount mechanism (see below). The rediscount rate (r_d) measures the cost of reserves obtained in this manner. Thus,

$$r_t = r_t'(r_{bp} - r_t, r_{bf} - r_t, r_d). \tag{2.84}$$

Simplifying,

$$r_t = r_t(r_{bp}, r_{bf}, r_d). \tag{2.85}$$

The explicit form of 2.85 is

$$r_t = r_{tt-1} + a(\bar{L}_b - L_{bp}^D - L_{bf}^D) \tag{2.86}$$

where $1 > a > 0$. Increases in r_{bf} or r_{bp} make loans more profitable and thus induce the banks to attempt to attract more time deposits by raising r_t and vice versa. Increases in the rediscount rate tend to reduce rediscounting and thus induce the bank to look elsewhere for reserves to make up for the drop in rediscounting.

Demand deposits do not earn a monetary return. Service charges are ignored. The banks accept all demand deposits offered them. Thus, the banks' demand for demand deposits is perfectly elastic. Letting D^D represent the banks' demand for demand deposits, we have

$$D^D = D_p^S + D_f^S + D_n^S. \tag{2.87}$$

The total amount of demand deposits in t, D_t, is given by

$$D_t \equiv D_t^D = D_{pt}^S + D_{ft}^S + D_{nt}^S. \tag{2.88}$$

Demand and time deposits are the only liabilities of the bank that will be given explicit treatment.[2] The only explicit recognition of capital account items is the assumption that all profits are paid out to the banks' owners.

Loans, Reserves, and Rediscounting

The legal reserve requirement, r, applies to both demand and time deposits. The total level of required reserves in period t, R_t, is given by

$$R_t = r_t(D_t + T_t). \tag{2.89}$$

Required services are all held in the form of noninterest-bearing deposits at the monetary authority. For simplicity, vault cash, or cash held by the banks, is not assumed to be part of required, or primary, reserves.

Secondary reserves are held in three forms—cash, securities issued by

2. Banks are assumed not to hold demand deposits in other banks. This in effect eliminates the correspondent banking system from consideration in the model.

firms, and government securities. Desired cash balances, C_b, are given by

$$C_b = \gamma(D + T) \tag{2.90}$$

where $1 > \gamma > 0$. Interest rates are omitted from 2.90, reflecting the assumption that banks hold vault cash strictly to meet day-to-day withdrawal requirements, and that any cash over the minimum needed for these requirements will be used to buy government securities as long as r_g is greater than zero. This is equivalent to assuming that the banks do not have a speculative demand for money, in this case, cash.

The desired level of government securities, G_b, is given by

$$G_b = \rho(D + T) + A_{10}\bar{r}_b, \tag{2.91}$$

where ρ is a positive constant less than 1. Its magnitude is determined by the "institutional" requirements for secondary reserves, such as seasonal fluctuations in deposits, etc. a_{10} is a positive constant reflecting two assumptions: that as the yield on government securities increases, these securities become a more attractive form in which to hold secondary reserves—e.g., an increase in r_g causes a larger portion of secondary reserves to be held in government securities, ceteris paribus; and that an increase in r_g also causes the total amount of desired secondary reserves to increase, ceteris paribus. b_{10} is a negative constant reflecting the fact that secondary reserves will be switched from government's to firms' securities as the yield on these securities rises, ceteris paribus. f_{10}, d_{10}, and e_{10} are also negative constants reflecting two assumptions: that as r_t rises, profit margins are squeezed, inducing the banks to shift funds from low-yielding secondary reserves to higher-yielding loans; and that as the rates banks charge for loans increase (r_{bp} and r_{bf}), the increased profitability of loans also tends to reduce the level of desired secondary reserves. The converses of the above assumptions are also assumed to hold.

The desired level of firms' securities, F_b, is given by

$$F_b = \mu(D + T) + A_{11}\bar{r}_b. \tag{2.92}$$

μ is a positive constant less than 1. a_{11} is a negative constant while b_{11} is positive. f_{11}, d_{11}, and e_{11} are also negative constants. The arguments here are the same as those given for the signs of the constant terms in 2.91 above.

The total level of desired secondary reserves is given by the sum of 2.90, 2.91, and 2.92. At no time will the actual level of secondary reserves be less than the desired level. If, however, the banks are unable to make the total amount of loans they wish, actual secondary reserves may be greater than the desired level. Letting R_t^{Sa} be actual secondary reserves in t,

$$R_t^{Sa} = C_{bt} + G_{bt} + F_{bt} + (L_t^S - L_t) \tag{2.93}$$

where L_t^S is the total quantity of loans banks wish to make in t and L_t the amount actually lent by the banks in t. The term in the parentheses in 2.93 will be referred to as surplus reserves. It is assumed that all surplus reserves are held in the form of cash so that the banks' actual cash holdings in t are given by

$$C_{bt}^a = C_{bt} + L_t^S - L_t \tag{2.94}$$

when $L_t^S - L_t$ is positive.

$$C_{bt}^a = C_{bt} \tag{2.95}$$

when $L_t^S = L_t$. Surplus reserves are assumed to be held in cash rather than securities to reflect their transitory nature. That is, banks feel that such a situation is only temporary and do not wish to switch in and out of securities on a short-run, unpredictable basis.[3]

Bank loans to both the public and firms are made for a period of n years. Loans made in period t carry a rate of interest of r_{bpt} and r_{bft}, respectively. The proceeds to the bank of a loan of X dollars are $(1 + r_b)X$, repaid in n installments of $(1 + r_b)X/n$ dollars. Loans to both the public and the firms are assumed to be riskless. (Alternatively, one could think of r_{bpt} and r_{bft} as representing the net return per dollar lent after default and added collection expenses.)

The aggregate amount banks wish to loan from unborrowed reserves in t is given by

$$\bar{L}_t^S = \pi(D_t + T_t) + A_{12}\bar{r}_b. \tag{2.96}$$

3. In an attempt to keep the model as simple as possible, we have omitted the Federal Funds market, although it is recognized that this is the sort of situation that created this particular financial market.

π is a positive constant less than 1. a_{12} and b_{12} are negative constants since increased yields on securities will, ceteris paribus, tend to reduce loans and increase secondary reserves. d_{12} is a positive constant since increased costs create pressure for shifting from secondary reserves to loans. f_{12} and e_{12} are positive, reflecting the fact that the increased profitability of loans as interest rates rise will result in increased willingness to lend. Surplus reserves in period $t-1$ ($C_{bt-1}^a - C_{bt-1}$) clearly increase the banks' willingness to lend. The amounts banks wish to loan to the public and to firms, $\bar{L}_{pt}^{Sb}$ and $\bar{L}_{ft}^{Sb}$, depend on $\bar{L}_t^S$, the difference between r_{bpt} and r_{bft}, and institutional factors:

$$\bar{L}_{pt}^{Sb} = \ell_p^b \bar{L}_t^S + a_{13}(r_{bpt} - r_{bft}) \tag{2.97}$$

$$\bar{L}_{ft}^{Sb} = \ell_f^b \bar{L}_t^S - a_{13}(r_{bpt} - r_{bft}) \tag{2.98}$$

where $\ell_p^b + \ell_f^b = 1$ and a_{13} is a positive constant. Institutional factors, such as the desire to meet the demands of existing customers, unwillingness to loan more or less than some percentages of the total loan portfolio to any one type of borrower, etc., determine the relative sizes of ℓ_p^b and ℓ_f^b as well as the absolute size of a_{13}. The smaller a_{13} is, the more r_{bp} and r_{bf} must differ to induce a wide difference between $\bar{L}_{pt}^{Sb}$ and $\bar{L}_{ft}^{Sb}$.

$\bar{L}_{pt}^{Sb}$ and $\bar{L}_{ft}^{Sb}$ represent the initial quantity of loans the banks are willing to supply the public and the firms from unborrowed reserves. These figures do not necessarily represent the actual amount of loans made. Let $\bar{L}_{pt}^{Db}$ and $\bar{L}_{ft}^{Db}$ represent the quantity of bank loans demanded by the public and the firms in period t. The actual amount of bank loans made to each sector in period t, L_{pt}^b and L_{ft}^b, depends on the quantities demanded and the quantities supplied from unborrowed reserves as well as the banks' willingness to engage in, and ability to obtain, rediscounting.

When $\bar{L}_{pt}^{Sb} + \bar{L}_{ft}^{Sb} \geq \bar{L}_{pt}^{Db} + \bar{L}_{ft}^{Db}$, no rediscounting occurs. In this case the final amounts lent are given by

$$L_{pt}^b = L_{pt}^{Db} \tag{2.99}$$

$$L_{ft}^b = L_{ft}^{Db}. \tag{2.100}$$

This situation is illustrated in Table 1.

In this case, even though $\bar{L}_{pt}^{Db} > \bar{L}_{pt}^{Sb}$, the entire public loan demand was satisfied by shifting a portion of the initial (and unlent) allocation for loans to firms over to public loans. Firms were also able to borrow the amount they wished.

TABLE 1. $\bar{L}_{pt}^{Sb} + \bar{L}_{ft}^{Sb} \geq \bar{L}_{pt}^{Db} + \bar{L}_{ft}^{Db}$

$\bar{L}_{pt}^{Sb}$ = $100	$\bar{L}_{pt}^{Db}$ = $125	L_{pt}^{b} = $125
$\bar{L}_{ft}^{Sb}$ = $200	$\bar{L}_{ft}^{Db}$ = $160	L_{ft}^{b} = $160
$\bar{L}_{pt}^{Sb} + \bar{L}_{ft}^{Sb}$ = $300	$\bar{L}_{pt}^{Db} + \bar{L}_{ft}^{Db}$ = $285	$L_{pt}^{b} + L_{ft}^{b}$ = $285

When $\bar{L}_{pt}^{Sb} + \bar{L}_{ft}^{Sb} < \bar{L}_{pt}^{Db} + \bar{L}_{ft}^{Db}$ the final amounts lent depend on the amount of rediscounting. The banks' total demand for rediscounting is given by

$$d_t^d = \bar{L}_{pt}^{Db} + \bar{L}_{ft}^{Db} - (\bar{L}_{pt}^{Sb} + \bar{L}_{ft}^{Sb}) - d_o \left(\frac{1}{r_{bpt} - r_{dt}} \right)$$

$$- d_1 \left(\frac{1}{r_{bft} - r_{dt}} \right). \tag{2.101}$$

It is convenient to decompose 2.101 into the banks' demand for rediscounting to make additional loans to the public, d_o^d, and to make additional loans to firms, d_1^d.

$$d_{ot}^d = \bar{L}_{pt}^{Db} - \bar{L}_{pt}^{Sb} - (\bar{L}_{ft}^{Sb} - \bar{L}_{ft}^{Db}) - \frac{d_o}{r_{bpt} - r_{dt}} \tag{2.102}$$

$$d_{lt}^d = \bar{L}_{ft}^{Db} - \bar{L}_{ft}^{Sb} - (\bar{L}_{pt}^{Sb} - \bar{L}_{pt}^{Db}) - \frac{d_1}{r_{bft} - r_{dt}} \tag{2.103}$$

where

$$d_{ot}^d + d_{lt}^d = d_t^d. \tag{2.104}$$

The terms $-(\bar{L}_{ft}^{Sb} - \bar{L}_{ft}^{Db})$ in 2.102 and $-(\bar{L}_{pt}^{Sb} - \bar{L}_{pt}^{Db})$ in 2.103 enter these equations only when they are negative, that is, only when the quantity of loans demanded by one sector is smaller than the quantity the banks are willing to lend to that sector. This situation allows the banks to "shift" more funds in amounts equal to $-(\overline{L}_{ft}^{Sb} - \overline{L}_{ft}^{Db})$ or $-(\overline{L}_{pt}^{Sb} - \overline{L}_{pt}^{Db})$ to the other sector, thus reducing the banks' demand for rediscounting.

The parameters d_o and d_1 are positive and assumed to be greater than 1. Their sizes determine how responsive the demand for discounting is to differences between the rate(s) of interest on loans and the rediscount rate. The closer r_d comes to $r_{bp}(r_{bf})$, the greater is $d_o/r_{bpt} - r_{dt}(d_1/r_{bft} - r_{dt})$ and the smaller is the amount of discounting the banks are willing to engage in. Note that the constructions of 2.102 and 2.103 imply that the amount of rediscounting will not be sufficient to meet the entire excess demand for loans. The addition of a constant term to these equations would make this possible for certain combinations of the loan rates and the rediscount rate. These terms have been omitted to reflect more strongly the banks' assumed reluctance to engage in rediscounting.

Based on the previous assumption, the actual amount of rediscounting is always equal to the amount of discounting demanded:

$$d_t \equiv d_t^d = d_{ot}^d + d_{lt}^d. \tag{2.105}$$

We shall use the terms d_{ot}^d and d_{lt}^d to stand for both the quantities of rediscounting demand as well as the amounts of rediscounting made because of the excess demand for loans from either the public (d_{ot}^d) or the firms (d_{lt}^d) in period t. Thus, in the case where $\overline{L}_{pt}^{Sb} + \overline{L}_{ft}^{Sb} < \overline{L}_{pt}^{Db} + \overline{L}_{ft}^{Db}$, the actual amounts lent to each sector, L_{pt}^b and L_{ft}^b, are given by

$$L_{pt}^b = \min \left\{ \overline{L}_{pt}^{Db}, \overline{L}_{pt}^{Sb} + (\overline{L}_{ft}^{Sb} - \overline{L}_{ft}^{Db}) + d_{ot}^d \right\} \tag{2.106}$$

and

$$L_{ft}^b = \min \left\{ \overline{L}_{ft}^{Db}, \overline{L}_{ft}^{Sb} + (\overline{L}_{pt}^{Sb} - \overline{L}_{pt}^{Db}) + d_{lt}^d \right\}. \tag{2.107}$$

Note that the terms $\overline{L}_{-t}^{Sb} - \overline{L}_{-t}^{Db}$ do not enter 2.106 and 2.107 if they are negative. In the case being considered, only one of these terms may be positive, although both may be negative. In that event, the corresponding rediscount term will be zero. Table 2 illustrates the situation in which one of these terms is positive while the other is negative. Equations 2.106 and 2.107 can also be used to express the final amounts lent when $\bar{L}_f^{Sb} + \bar{L}_p^{Sb} \geq \bar{L}_p^{Db} + \bar{L}_f^{Db}$, since neither type of borrower can be induced to borrow more than the quantity of loans he initially demands ($\bar{L}_p^{Db}$ or $\bar{L}_f^{Db}$). Equations 2.99 and 2.100 express this in much simpler form than the more general relationships 2.106 and 2.107.

TABLE 2. $\bar{L}_f^S - \bar{L}_f^D < 0, \bar{L}_p^S - \bar{L}_p^D > 0$

$\bar{L}_f^S = 100$	$\bar{L}_f^D = 150$	$\bar{L}_f^S - \bar{L}_f^D = -50$
$\bar{L}_p^S = 100$	$\bar{L}_p^D = 90$	$\bar{L}_p^S - \bar{L}_p^D = 10$
$\bar{L}_f^S + \bar{L}_p^S = 200 \quad < $	$\bar{L}_f^D + \bar{L}_p^D = 240$	

$$d_o^d = 90 - 100 - (100 - 150) - \frac{d_o}{r_{bp} - r_d}$$

$$= -10 - 0 - \frac{d_o}{r_{bp} - r_{dt}} < 0 = 0$$

$$d_1^d = 150 - 100 - (100 - 90) - \frac{d_1}{r_{bf} - r_d}$$

$$= 50 - 10 - \frac{d_1}{r_{bf} - r_d} = \text{(by assumption on } d_1, r_{bf}, r_d) = 35$$

$$L_{pt}^b = \min \{90, 100\} + (100 - 150)$$
$$+ 0$$
$$= \min 90, 100 + 0 = 90 = \bar{L}_p^D$$

$$L_{ft}^b = \min \{150 - 100\} + (100 - 90)$$
$$+ 35$$
$$= 100 + 10 + 35 = 145 \ \bar{L}_{ft}^{Db}$$

The rates of interest on bank loans in t are given by

$$r_{bpt} = r_{bpt-1} + a_p(\bar{L}_{pt-1}^{Db} - \bar{L}_{pt-1}^{Sb}) +$$
$$b_p(r_{bpt-1} - r_{npt-1}) \tag{2.108}$$

$$r_{bft} = r_{bft-1} + a_f(\bar{L}_{ft-1}^{Db} - \bar{L}_{ft-1}^{Sb}) +$$
$$b_f(r_{bft-1} - r_{nft-1}) \tag{2.109}$$

where a_p and a_f are positive constants. These equations embody this conceptualization: At the beginning of period t, banks adjust their rates either up or down, depending on whether there was an excess demand $(\bar{L}^{Db}_{-t-1} - \bar{L}^{Sb}_{-t-1} > 0)$ or an excess supply of loans $(\bar{L}^{Db}_{-t-1} - \bar{L}^{Sb}_{-t-1} < 0)$ in the previous period. The amount of the adjustment depends not only on the size of the previous excess supply or demand, but also on the sizes of a_p and a_f. Other rates of interest are not explicitly included in 2.108 and 2.109, as their impact on r_{bp} and r_{bf} is contained in the terms $\bar{L}^{Db}$ and $\bar{L}^{Sb}$.

Concluding this section we have the simple statement that the banks' assets and liabilities must be equal.

$$T_t + D_t = C_{bt} + G_{bt} + F_{bt} + R_t + \sum_{i=t-n}^{t} L_i^b -$$

$$\sum_{i=t-n}^{t} d_i. \tag{2.110}$$

The banks' income statement in period t is more complex as it must take into account the effects of rediscounting on loan profitability and the possibility of capital gains or losses incurred on government and firms' securities. Let $\pi_{\varrho p1}$ represent the total stream of profits from loans made in period 1 at maturity. Then, without rediscounting, under the assumption of no default,

$$\pi_{\varrho p1} = (1 + r_{bp1}) L_{p1} - L_{p1} = r_{bp1} L_{p1}. \tag{2.111}$$

The profit from loans made in period 1 in any one period, again without discounting, is simply

$$\frac{(1 + r_{b1}) L_{p1}}{n} - \frac{L_{p1}}{n} = \frac{r_{bp1} L_{p1}}{n}. \tag{2.112}$$

The total stream of profits at maturity from loans made in period 1, given that a portion of them are rediscounted in periods after period 1, is given by

$$\pi_{\varrho 1} = \frac{m}{n} (1 + r_{b1}) L_1 + d_{m+1,1} + [(\frac{n-m}{n})(1 + r_{b1})]$$

$$[L_1 - \frac{nd_{m+1,1}}{(n-m)(1 - rd_{m+1})(1 + r_{b1})}] - L_1 \tag{2.113}$$

where $\frac{m}{n} (1 + r_{b1}) L_1$ gives the repayment of interest and principal received by the bank prior to rediscounting a portion of L_1; $d_{m+1,1}$ is the proceeds of rediscounting a portion of L_1 in period m + 1;

$(\frac{n - m}{n})(1 + r_{b1})$ $[L_1 - nd_{m + 1, 1}/(n - m)(1 - rd_{m + 1})(1 + r_{b1})] - L_1$
is the repayment of interest and principal of the portion of L_1 *not*
rediscounted in period $m + 1$; and L_1 is simply the face value of the loans
made in period 1. Equation 2.113 reduces to

$$\pi_{\mathcal{Q}1} = r_{b1}L_1 + d_{m + 1, 1} [1 - \frac{1}{1 - rd_{m + 1}}]. \tag{2.114}$$

The last term in 2.114 will be negative since $0 < 1 - rd_{m + 1} < 1$ and
measures the loss of profit on L_1 loans caused by rediscounting a
portion of them.

Profit on L_1 loans for the period in which they are rediscounted is
given by

$$\pi_{\mathcal{Q}1}^{m + 1} = [L_1 - \frac{nd_{m + 1, 1}}{(n - m)(1 + r_{b1})(1 - rd_{m + 1})}] (\frac{1 + r_{b1}}{n})$$

$$- [L_1 - \frac{nd_{m + 1, 1}}{(n - m)(1 + r_{b1})(1 - rd_{m + 1})}] (\frac{1}{n}) + d_{m + 1, 1}$$

$$[1 - \frac{1}{1 - rd_{m + 1}}] \tag{2.115}$$

which reduces to

$$\pi_{\mathcal{Q}1}^{m + 1} = \frac{r_{b1}L_1}{n} + d_{m + 1, 1} [1 + \frac{1}{(n - m)(1 + r_{b1})(1 - rd_{m + 1})} -$$

$$\frac{1}{(n - m)(1 - rd_{m + 1})} - \frac{1}{1 + rd_{m + 1}}]. \tag{2.116}$$

When no rediscounting occurs ($d_{m + 1, 1} = 0$), 2.116 is obviously equivalent to 2.111. Equation 2.116 serves as the basis for expressing the
profit from all loans in any one period. Letting $\overline{d}_{ji}$ represent the
unrepaid principal and interest of a jth period loan rediscounted in
period i, we have

$$\pi_{\mathcal{Q}}^{m + 1} = \sum_{j = m + 1 - n}^{m + 1} [\frac{r_{bj}i > j(L_j - \sum_{i = m - n}^{m} \overline{d}_{ji})}{n}$$

$$+ d_{m + 1, j} (1 + \frac{1}{(n - m)(1 + r_{bj})(1 - rd_{m + 1})} -$$

$$\frac{1}{(n - m)(1 - rd_{m + 1})} - \frac{1}{1 - rd_{m + 1}})] .\tag{2.117}$$

Profits on loans to the public, $\pi_{\ell p}^{m + 1}$, is given by using r_{bpj}, d_{pji}, and $d_{pm + 1, j}$ in 2.117, while π_f is obtained by using the corresponding rate and rediscounting measures for loans to the firms. Thus,

$$\pi_\ell^{m + 1} = \pi_{\ell p}^{m + 1} + \pi_{\ell f}^{m + 1} .\tag{2.118}$$

Profit in period m + 1 from government securities, $\pi_g^{m + 1}$, is simply

$$\pi_g^{m + 1} = r_{gm + 1} G_{bm + 1} .\tag{2.119}$$

No capital gains or losses are made on government securities as a result of the assumptions of one-year maturity and no intraperiod trading of the securities by the banks.

Profit in m + 1 from firms' securities, $\pi_f^{m + 1}$, includes both interest and possible capital gains (losses). Thus,

$$\pi_f^{m + 1} = \sum_{i = m + 1 - k}^{m + 1} \frac{r_{fi} B_{bfi}}{k} + \sum_{i = m - k}^{m + 1}$$

$$(P_{bfm + 1} - P_{bfi}) (F_{bfm + 1} - F_{bfi})\tag{2.120}$$

where k is the maturity of the firms' bonds and $F_{bfm + 1} - F_{bfi}$ does not enter the equation unless it is negative, e.g., unless the banks actually sell period i bonds in m + 1 to actually realize accrued capital gains or losses.

The banks' overall gross profit (before payments to owners, purchase of factors, and payment of interest on time deposits) in m + 1, $\pi^{m + 1}$, is given by

$$\pi_b^{m + 1} = \pi_{\ell p}^{m + 1} + \pi_{\ell f}^{m + 1} + \pi_g^{m + 1} + \pi_f^{m + 1} .\tag{2.121}$$

The only portion of $\pi^{m + 1}$ that is not received directly by the public in the form of income in m + 1 is the portion used to purchase capital, $P_{km + 1} X_{kbm + 1}$. Thus, the banks' contribution to the public's income in m + 1, $Y_b^{m + 1}$, is

$$Y_b^{m + 1} = \pi_b^{m + 1} - P_{km + 1} X_{kbm + 1} .\tag{2.122}$$

The Nonbank Financial Sector (Intermediaries)

The nonbank financial sector is assumed to have two major functions. It accepts deposits from the public and the firms and lends to each of these sectors. The insurance function of this sector will not be explicitly recognized. Rather, deposits will be taken to include not only the typical savings deposit at, say, a savings and loan institution but also insurance premiums. Payments on insurance claims will be included in any withdrawals of principal plus interest from the "savings" accounts. For simplicity, it is further assumed that the rates of interest paid on these deposits are the same for the public and the firms. The deposits in the nonbank financial sector are not assumed to be part of the stock of money. With the submersion of the insurance function, the major impact of the nonbank financial sector will be on the banking sector with which it competes both for deposits and for loans.

The following relations describe the aggregate activities of the nonbank financial sector.

$$N = N^S \equiv N^D. \tag{2.123}$$

The actual level of deposits, N, is identically equal to the demand by the firms and the public for them, i.e., the supply of deposits is perfectly elastic.

$$N = L_f^n + L_p^n + G_n + D_n + B_n + C_n + T_n. \tag{2.124}$$

This is simply the balance sheet equation for the nonbank financial sector. Note that 2.124 reflects the assumption that the nonbank sector has no direct connection with the banks except to hold demand deposits and time deposits.

$$\bar{L}_n^S = \ell_n N + A_{14} \bar{r}_n \tag{2.125}$$

$$G_n^D = g_n N + A_{15} \bar{r}_n \tag{2.126}$$

$$D_n^D = d_n N + A_{16} \bar{r}_n \tag{2.127}$$

$$F_n^D = b_n N + A_{17} \bar{r}_n \tag{2.128}$$

$$C_n^D = c_n N. \tag{2.129}$$

Equations 2.125 through 2.129 are the basic decision functions of the nonbank sector. Equation 2.125 gives the maximum aggregate amount of loans the sector is willing to make while 2.126 to 2.129 represent the demand for nonloan assets, given that the nonbank sector is able to loan all it desires. Insufficient demand for loans will result in additional holdings of government securities, firms' securities, cash, and demand deposits as specified below. ℓ_n, g_n, d_n, b_n, and c_n are positive constants, while r_{np} is the rate of interest on loans to the public, r_{nf} the rate on loans to the firms, and r_f the rate paid on deposits. All other symbols are as defined previously.

The aggregate amount willing to be lent, L_n^S, is broken down between the firms and public in a manner analogous to that of the banks.

$$\bar{L}_{pt}^{Sn} = \ell_p^n L_t^{Sn} + a_{18} \left(r_{npt} - r_{nft} \right) \tag{2.130}$$

$$\bar{L}_{ft}^{Sn} = \ell_f^n L_t^{Sn} - a_{18} \left(r_{npt} - r_{nft} \right) \tag{2.131}$$

$$\bar{L}_{pt}^{Sn} + \bar{L}_{ft}^{Sn} = L_t^{Sn}. \tag{2.132}$$

Equations 2.130 and 2.131 are analogous to 2.97 and 2.98 for the banking sector. ℓ_p^n and ℓ_f^n represent institutional factors influencing the desired distribution of loans between the public and firms. $\ell_p^n + \ell_f^n = 1$. a_{18} is a positive constant whose size determines the importance of interest rate differences in loan distribution.

Adjustments in the initial breakdown occur if either the public's or the firms' demand for loans from the nonbank sector is less than the initial amount the nonbank sector is willing to lend while the demand from the other sector is greater than the initial amount. Thus, if $L_{np}^D < \bar{L}_{np}^S$ and $L_{nf}^D > \bar{L}_{nf}^S$, then L_{np}, the actual amount lent to the public, is equal to L_{np}^D and $L_{nf}^S = \min \left(\bar{L}_{nf}^S + \bar{L}_{np}^S - L_{np}^D, L_n^S - L_{np}^D \right)$. Similarly, if $L_{np}^D > \bar{L}_{np}^S$ and $L_{np}^D < \bar{L}_{nf}^S$ then $L_{np}^S = \min \left(\bar{L}_{np}^S + \bar{L}_{nf}^S - L_{nf}^D, L_n^S - L_{nf}^D \right)$. In either case the amounts actually lent in each sector are given by

$$L_{np} = \min \ \left\{ L_{np}^S + (\bar{L}_f^{Sn} - L_f^{Dn}), L_{np}^D \right\} \tag{2.133}$$

and

$$L_{nf} = \min \ \left\{ L_{nf}^S + (\bar{L}_p^{Sn} + L_p^{Dn}), L_{nf}^S \right\}. \tag{2.134}$$

The total amount lent, L_n, is simply the sum of 2.133 and 2.134. In no case can L_n be larger than L_n^S. It may, however, be smaller. In this case the holdings of interest earning assets are increased above the levels given by 2.75 through 2.127 as given below.

$$L_n^S - L_n = \Delta G_n^D \text{ if } r_g > r_t, r_f \tag{2.135}$$

$$L_n^S - L_n = \Delta B_f^D \text{ if } r_f > r_t, r_g \tag{2.136}$$

$$L_n^S - L_n = \Delta T_f^D \text{ if } r_t > r_g, r_f. \tag{2.137}$$

If two of the rates (r_g, r_t, r_f) are equal and the third smaller, the increase in demand for those assets will be equal to one-half of $L_n^S - L_n$. If all three rates are equal, the increase in demand for each asset will equal one-third of $L_n^S - L_n$. Since the supplies of government securities and time deposits are assumed to be perfectly elastic, no complications arise if either 2.135 or 2.137 hold. If 2.136 holds, it is possible that, since the supply of firms' securities is not perfectly elastic, the nonbank sector may not be able to acquire all the firms' securities it desires. In this case, either government securities or time deposits will be increased in an amount equal to the unsatisfied demand for firms' securities, depending on the relative sizes of r_g and r_t.

To describe the determination of the various rates of interest associated with the nonbank sector, we again introduce the subscript t to represent time. Note that this subscript has been omitted from the first fifteen equations merely for convenience. We have

$$r_{nft+1} = r_{nft} + a_{19}(L_{nft}^{Sn} - L_{ft}^{Dn}) + b_{19}(r_{nft} - r_{bft}) \tag{2.138}$$

where $a_{19} > 0$ and $b_{19} < 0$.

$$r_{npt+1} = r_{npt} + a_{20}(L_{npt}^S - L_{npt}^D) + b_{20}(r_{npt} - r_{bpt}) \tag{2.139}$$

where $a_{20} > 0$ and $b_{20} < 0$.

$$r_{nt+1} = r_{nt} + a_{21}(L_n^S - L_{np}^D - L_{nf}^D) \tag{2.140}$$

where $a_{21}, b_{21} < 0$.

For the nonbank sector to be in equilibrium these conditions must be satisfied:

$$r_{nt+i} = r_{nt+i-1} \tag{2.141}$$

$$r_{nft+i} = r_{nft+i-1} \tag{2.142}$$

$$r_{npt+i} = r_{npt+i-1} \tag{2.143}$$

$$L_{nt}^S = L_{nt} \tag{2.144}$$

$$F_t = F_t^D. \tag{2.145}$$

Note that desired holdings of time and demand deposits, government securities, and cash will be satisfied under all conditions.

The intermediaries' "balance sheet" was given in Equation 2.124. Their "income statement" provides Y_n, the contribution of the intermediaries to the income of the public in period t. For simplicity, it is assumed that all loans made by the intermediaries have a maturity of n years. Since we do not provide for any governmental sources of reserves for the intermediaries (no rediscounting of their loans), the profit on loans in period t, $\pi_{\ell n}^t$, is simply

$$\pi_{\ell n}^t = \sum_{i=t-n-1}^{t-1} \left(\frac{r_{npi} L_{pi}^n}{n} \right) + \sum_{i=t-n-1}^{t-1}$$

$$\left(\frac{r_{nfi} L_{fi}^n}{n} \right). \tag{2.146}$$

Profit on government securities in t, π_{gn}^t, is given by

$$\pi_{gn}^t = r_{gt} G_{nt}. \tag{2.147}$$

Profit on firms' securities is

$$\pi_{fn}^t = \sum_{i=m+1-k}^{m+1} \frac{r_{fi} B_{nfi}}{k} + \sum_{i=m-k}^{m+1}$$

$$(P_{bfm+1} - P_{bfi})(B_{nfm+1} - B_{nfi}) \tag{2.148}$$

which is equivalent to 2.120. The intermediaries' gross profit in t, π_n^t, is

$$\pi_n^t = \pi_{\ell n}^t + \pi_{gn}^t + \pi_{fn}^t. \tag{2.149}$$

The only portion of π_n^t not received directly by the public in the form of interest payments, labor payments, or dividends is the portion used to purchase the capital good, $P_{kt}X_{knt}$. Thus,

$$Y_n^t = \pi_n^t - P_{kt}X_{knt}. \tag{2.150}$$

THE PUBLIC SECTOR (HOUSEHOLDS)

The public sector is composed of all individuals in the economy acting in their roles as consumers and suppliers of factors. Only the aggregate behavior of this sector is considered; no attempt is made to distinguish among different individuals or groups of individuals.

The basic relationships for the public sector are:

$$D_{pt} = k_1 Y_t + A_{22}\bar{r}_p \tag{2.151}$$

$$C_{pt} = k_2 Y_t + A_{23}\bar{r}_p \tag{2.152}$$

$$T_{pt} = k_3 Y_t + A_{24}\bar{r}_p \tag{2.153}$$

$$C_{nt} = cY_t + A_{25}\bar{r}_p \tag{2.154}$$

$$G_{pt} = gY_t + A_{26}\bar{r}_p \tag{2.155}$$

$$L_{pt}^{Db} = \ell_p^b Y_t + A_{27}\bar{r}_p + (L_{pt-1}^b - L_{pt-1}^{Db}) \tag{2.156}$$

$$L_{pt}^{Dn} = \ell_p^n Y_t + A_{28}\bar{r}_p + (L_{pt-1}^n - L_{pt-1}^{Dn}) \tag{2.157}$$

$$F_{pt} = f_p Y_t + A_{29}\bar{r}_p \tag{2.158}$$

$$N_{pt} = n_p Y_t + A_{30}\bar{r}_p \tag{2.159}$$

Equations 2.151 through 2.159 express the public's demand for demand deposits, currency, time deposits, the consumption good, government securities, loans, and firms' securities in dollar terms. P_c is not only the price of the consumption good but, since there is by assumption only one composite consumer good, it also serves as the consumers' price index.

Equations 2.151 through 2.153 require no further comment. Equation 2.154 expresses the dollar value of the public's *purchases* of the consumer good, e.g., $C_{nt} = P_{ct}X_{cpt}$. It does not include the value of the consumer good transferred to the public sector by the government. Total consumption by the public sector of X_c in period t is given by $C_{nt} + P_{ct}X_{cgt}$ (see the section on the government sector).

Equations 2.156 and 2.157 express the public's demand for loans; their sum is the aggregate demand. It is assumed, for simplicity, that an unsatisfied demand for loans from one sector will not increase the quantity of loans the public demands from the other sector in the same time period. Unsatisfied loan demand in t causes the quantity of loans demanded in t + 1 to increase by an amount equal to the excess demand.

Equations 2.155 and 2.158 are self-explanatory.

Other relations for the public sector include: (1) the definition of the public's gross income, $\bar{Y}_t$:

$$\bar{Y}_t = Y_{gt} + Y_{bt} + Y_{nt} + Y_{ft} + r_{gt}G_{pt} + r_{tt}T_{pt} +$$
$$r_{nt}N_{pt} + r_{ft}F_{pt}; \qquad (2.160)$$

(2) the definition of disposable income, Y_t:

$$Y_t = (1 - t)\bar{Y}_t; \qquad (2.161)$$

(see the section on the government sector).

THE MARKETS

In this section I attempt to connect the previous sections by examining the various markets in the model in greater detail and in isolation.

Currency Market

The price of currency is the opportunity cost of holding it, the income sacrificed by not holding a return-earning asset. For simplicity it is assumed that this cost can be represented by the largest of r_f, r_g, r_n, and r_t.[4] Thus, the price of currency for the public is equal to 1 + max

---

4. Perhaps a more theoretically aesthetic way of viewing P_c is this: The price of currency is the opportunity cost of holding currency rather than a return-earning asset, e.g., time deposits, deposits in intermediaries, government securities, and firm securities. Let O_c be this cost. Then $O_c = O_c(r_f, r_g, r_n, r_t)$ (deposit in intermediaries) where the function describes the return that could be earned on an extra

$\{r_f, r_g, r_n, r_t\}$ while for the firms it is $1 + \max \{r_g, r_n, r_t\}$ since firms do not, by assumption, hold debt instruments of other firms. P_c for the intermediaries is $1 + \max \{r_f, r_g, r_t\}$ while for the banks, P_c is $1 + \max \{r_f, r_g\}$ since banks hold neither time deposits nor deposits in intermediaries. If P_c is the price of currency, we have the typical downward-sloping demand curve. Equations 2.66, 2.90, 2.129, and 2.154 give the demand for currency explicitly. All variables in these equations except $\max \{r_f, r_g, r_n, r_t\}$ must be considered fixed when included in Figure 4. Increases in rates other than the maximum rate shift the demand curves downward, since narrowing the difference between interest rates makes the security with the higher rate relatively less attractive. Increases in Y, D + T, or $P_cX_c + P_kX_k$ shift the curve outward. Note that the demand curve gives the demand for changes in currency holdings. At prices lower than P_{co} the public (bank, firm, or intermediary) wants to increase its currency holdings, while at prices above P_{co}, it wants to reduce them. The stock demand for currency can be readily found by combining last period's stock, C_{t-1}, with the desired change in this period. Note that C_{t-1} establishes the lower limit for changes in currency holdings during period t, since the stock of currency cannot be negative.

---

dollar distributed in the same percentage as the present distribution between time deposits, government securities, and firms' securities. For each sector we have:

1. $O_{cp} = r_t \dfrac{T_p}{T_p + G_p + B_{fp} + N_p} + r_g \dfrac{G_p}{T_p + G_p + B_{fp} + N_p} +$

   $r_f \dfrac{B_{fp}}{T_p + G_p + B_{fp} + N_p} + \dfrac{r_nN_p}{T_p + G_p + B_{fp} + N_p}$

2. $O_{cb} = r_t \dfrac{T_b}{T_p + G_p + B_{fp}} + r_g \dfrac{G_b}{T_p + G_p + B_{fp}} + r_f \dfrac{B_{fb}}{T_p + G_p + B_{fp}}$

3. $O_{cf} = r_t \dfrac{T_f}{T_f + G_f} + r_g \dfrac{G_f}{T_f + G_f} + \dfrac{r_gN_f}{T_f + G_f + N_f}$

4. $O_{cn} = \dfrac{r_tT_n}{T_n + G_n + B_{fn}} + \dfrac{r_gG_n}{T_n + G_n + B_{fn}} + \dfrac{r_fB_{fn}}{T_n + G_n + B_{fn}}$

For simplicity we have chosen not to use this definition of O_c.

The supply of currency in this model is not independent of the demand for it, since by assumption we have the government passively issuing or absorbing currency in the aggregate amount demanded by the public, firms, and banks. Thus, we have

$$D(dC) \equiv S(dC) \tag{2.162}$$

for all P_c. This aggregate demand for currency is obtained by summing the four sectors' demands for currency. Equation 2.162 holds both for each sector and for the aggregate. Thus, the currency market is in perpetual equilibrium.

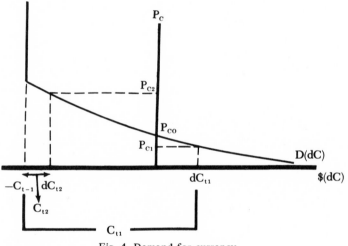

Fig. 4. Demand for currency

The Market for Demand Deposits

The price of demand deposits, P_D, is defined in the same way as the price of currency, i.e., $P_D = 1 + \max \{ r_f, r_g, r_n, r_t \}$ for the public, equal to $1 + \max \{ r_g, r_n, r_t \}$ for the firms, and equal to $1 + \max \{ r_f, r_g, r_t \}$ for the intermediaries. The demand for demand deposits can be viewed in the same way as the demands for currency, with the obvious exception that in this case there is, again by assumption, no bank demand for demand deposits. Figure 5 is analogous to Figure 4.

The banks are willing to accept any amount of new demand deposits and cannot prevent their withdrawal. Thus, again the supply of demand deposits is not independent of their demand, and we have

$$D(dD) \equiv S(dD) \tag{2.163}$$

for all P_D. The aggregate demand is the sum of the public's, firms', and intermediaries' demands and 2.163 holds for the aggregate market so that the market for demand deposits is also in perpetual equilibrium.

The Market for Time Deposits

The price of time deposits, P_t, is also an opportunity cost. Since time deposits earn a rate of return, the price of one dollar in time deposits, P_t, is given by

$$P_t = 1 + \max \left\{ r_f, r_g \right\} - r_t \text{ for the public,} \tag{2.164}$$

$$P_t = 1 + r_g - r_t \text{ for the firms, and} \tag{2.165}$$

$$P_t = 1 + \max \left\{ r_f, r_g \right\} - r_t \text{ for the intermediaries.} \tag{2.166}$$

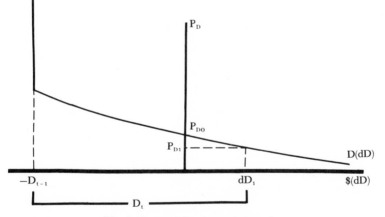

Fig. 5. Demand for demand deposits

The demand for time deposits is also analogous to the demand for currency and is shown in Figure 6. Summing over the public's, firms', and intermediaries' demands again yields the aggregate demand for time deposits. The banks again are assumed to be willing to supply an amount of time deposits and cannot prevent their withdrawal long enough to affect the analysis. Once again, then,

$$D(dT) \equiv S(dT) \tag{2.167}$$

for P_t and the aggregate market for time deposits is always in equilibrium.

The Market for Government Securities

This market is in all respects similar to the ones already described. We have

$$P_g = 1 + \max \left\{ r_f, r_t \right\} - r_g \text{ for the public;} \tag{2.168}$$

$$P_g = 1 + r_f - r_g \text{ for the banks;} \tag{2.169}$$

$$P_g = 1 + \max \left\{ r_n, r_t \right\} - r_g \text{ for the firms;} \tag{2.170}$$

$$P_g = 1 + \max \left\{ r_f, r_t \right\} - r_g \text{ for the intermediaries.} \tag{2.171}$$

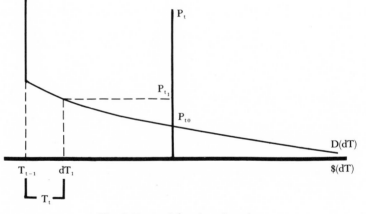

Fig. 6. Demand for time deposits

Then the demands can be shown in Figure 7. Aggregate demand is the sum of the four sectors' demands. The government is a passive supplier-absorber of government securities so that in each market and in the aggregate

$$D(dG) \equiv S(dG) \tag{2.172}$$

for all P_g. The market for government securities is always in equilibrium.

The Market for Bank Loans

This is the first market to boast a supply function that is independent of demand. The price of bank loans, P_ℓ, is $1 + r_{bp}$ for the public and $1 + r_{bf}$ for the firms. The demand for loans is again expressed in terms of desired changes in indebtedness to the banks. Thus, we have in general the situation shown in Figure 8. L_{t-1} is the total indebtedness to the bank (unpaid principal plus interest on loans) at the beginning of period t, and dL represents the change in indebtedness during t. Note that if $P_\ell = P_{\ell_0}$, the desired change in indebtedness is zero, but that this does not mean that desired new loans in t are also zero. When $P_\ell = P_{\ell_0}$, desired

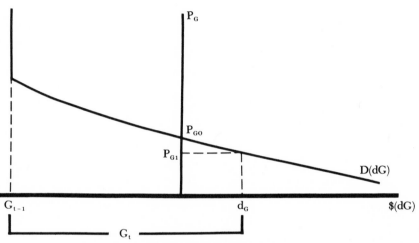

Fig. 7. Demand for government securities

loans in t are equal to $\int_0^t [1 + r_b(r)] L(r)dr/n$, the amount of loan repayments in t. Thus, desired new loans are zero when $P_\ell = P_{\ell_2}$ and the demand for loans is given by $D(d\ell)$ in Figure 8. A graph like Figure 8 exists both for firms and for the public. At any point in time the aggregate quantity of loans the banks are willing to supply is given by the solution to Equation 2.96. The supply of loans to each sector is based on the aggregate figure. The discussion in the section on the banking sector can be shown graphically as in Figure 9. Here Q_{spi} and Q_{sfi} represent the initial amounts desired to be loaned to the public and the firms as given by Equations 2.97 and 2.98. In the situation drawn in Figure 9, excess supply exists in both loan markets and the actual amount of loans made will be $QD_p + QD_f$. In the next period both rates

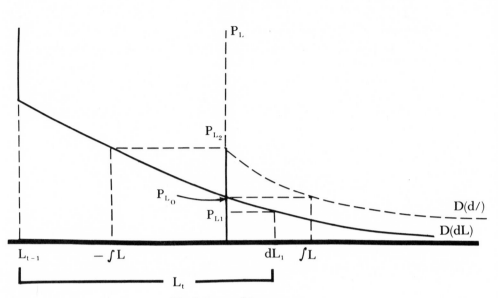

Fig. 8. Demand for bank loans

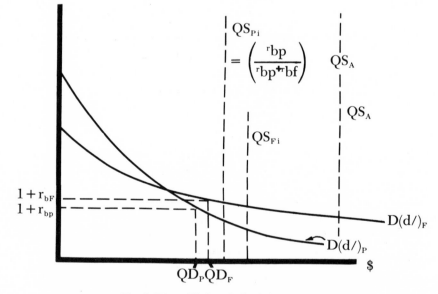

Fig. 9. Disequilibrium in bank-loan market

will be reduced. An equilibrium situation is shown in Figure 10. Not only do rates fall, but the aggregate amount of desired loans by the banks is also reduced.

Figure 11 is a graphical presentation of the adjustment occurring when there is excess demand in one market and excess supply in the other. Here QS_{ff} represents the final quantity of loans made to the firms and the two black arrows, ES_f, the final total excess supply of loans.

Equilibrium in the loan market clearly requires $QS_p = QD_r$, $QS_f = QD_f$, and $QD_p + QD_S = QS_a$. Equilibrium is achieved through adjustments of the rates of interest with its impact both on quantity demanded and quantity supplied.

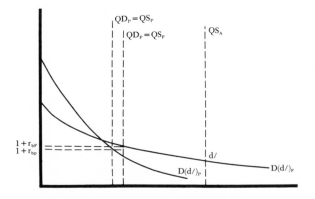

Fig. 10. Equilibrium in bank-loan market

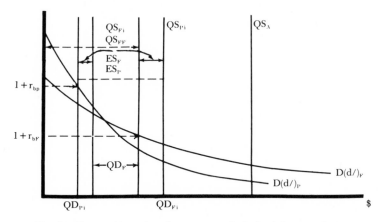

Fig. 11. Excess demand and excess supply in bank-loan market

The Market for Intermediary Loans

The analysis of the market for intermediary loans is identical to that given above for bank loans and will not be repeated.

The Market for the Capital Good

See the section on production, investment, and growth, and in particular Figure 2, for a discussion of the market for the capital good.

The Market for Firms' Securities

Debt instruments issued by the firms are held by the public, by intermediaries, and by banks. The price is again defined in an opportunity cost sense. Thus, P_f, the price of firms' securities, is taken to be:

$$P_f = 1 + \max\left\{r_f, r_n, r_t\right\} - r_f \text{ for the public;} \qquad (2.173)$$

$$P_f = 1 + r_g - r_f \text{ for the bank;} \qquad (2.174)$$

$$P_f = 1 + \max\left\{r_g, r_t\right\} - r_f \text{ for the intermediaries.} \qquad (2.175)$$

The demands can be shown by Figure 12, which is completely analogous to Figure 7 (the demand for changes in holdings of government securities). In each period, the supply of securities by the firms is given by the solution of Equation 2.40. The desired change in securities outstand-

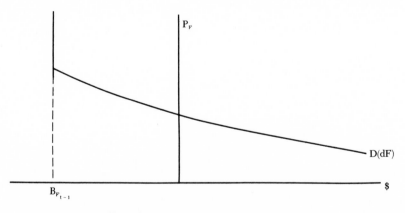

Fig. 12. Demand for firms' securities

ing can be represented by a vertical line. Thus, combining these flow demands and supplies we have, in the aggregate, Figure 13.

A Note on Aggregate Demands

Prices in the financial markets described have all been framed in terms of opportunity costs. This results in different prices for the same item in different sectors. For example, the price of government securities for the public is assumed to be $1 + \max \{r_f, r_t\} - r_g$ for the public, but $1 + \max \{r_t, r_n\} - r_g$ for the firms. If $r_f > r_t$, different prices result. When aggregating sector demands, the price is assumed to be $1/1 + r$, where r represents the rate on the item in question. This function does not contradict the sector prices since there is a one-to-one relationship between, for example, $1/1 + r_g$ and $1 + \max \{r_f, r_t\} - r_g$ and $1 + \max \{r_t, r_n\} - r_g$.

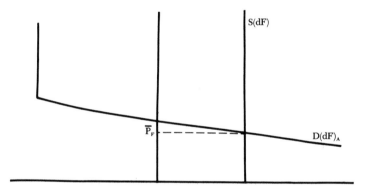

Fig. 13. Aggregate demand for firms' securities

RELATIONS OF THE MODEL

We reproduce simply the key relationships for each sector here for convenience.[5]

Production, Investment, and Growth

1. Aggregate production functions:

$$X_k^a = X_k(L_k, X_{kk}) \tag{2.1}$$

5. See Literature Cited, items 3, 20, 22, 25, 29, 37, 42, 43, 47, 53, 55, and 57 for a more complete discussion of some of the demand and supply functions presented here.

$$X_c^a = X_c(L_c, X_{kc}).$$ (2.3)

2. Transformation functions:

$$X_c = T(X_k)$$ (2.5)

$$X_{ci}^2 + X_{ki}^2 = \alpha_{ki}^2.$$ (2.9)

3. Full employment:

$X_i' = (X_{ci}', X_{ki}')$ is a full-employment output vector if

$$X_{ki}' = \sqrt{\alpha_{ki}^2 - X_{ci}'^2}, \; X_{ki}' \geq 0.$$ (2.10)

4. Rate of growth of the labor force:

$$\lambda = \lambda\left(\frac{dX_c}{dt}\right).$$ (2.13)

5. Stock demand for capital:

$$D_k = D_k(P_k, r, \emptyset).$$ (2.14)

6. Flow demand for capital:

$$dK = nK.$$ (2.15)

7. Stock supply of capital:

$$S_{kt} = K_t.$$

8. Flow supply of capital:

$$s_k = s_k(P_k).$$ (2.16)

9. Balanced growth:

$$\frac{\partial X_c}{\partial K_c} kK + \frac{\partial X_c}{\partial L_c} \lambda L = \frac{\partial X_k}{\partial K_k} kK + \frac{\partial X_k}{\partial L_k} \lambda L.$$ (2.30)

10. Supply of labor:

$$S^{\ell} = S^{\ell}(P_{\ell}, L).$$ (2.31)

11. Demand for labor:

$$D^{\ell} = MP_{\ell k}P_k + MP_{\ell c}PX_c + E.$$ (2.34)

The Firms

1. Desired level of retained earnings:

$$E_t^D = \alpha K_t + \beta I_{nt-1} + s[P_{ct}X_{ct} + P_{kt}X_{kt}] + \beta I_{nt-1}$$ (2.35)

$$E_t^D = f_3(K_t) - \beta(K_{t-1}).$$ (2.52)

2. Desired level of financing:

$$F_t^D = I_{nt} - \beta I_{nt-1}.$$ (2.36)

3. Demand for loans:

$$L_{ft}^{Db} = a_1(r_{bt}^f - r_{nt}^f) + b_1 L_{ft}^D$$ (2.43)

$$L_{ft}^{Dn} = a_2(r_{bt}^f - r_{nt}^f) + b_2 L_{ft}^D$$ (2.44)

$$L_{ft}^D = \ell_f F_t^D + A_3 \bar{r}_f.$$ (2.38)

4. Supply of securities:

$$F_t^S = b_f F_t^D + A_4 \bar{r}_f.$$ (2.40)

5. Desired change in retained earnings:

$$\Delta E_t^D = f_4(I_{nt-1}) - \beta(I_{nt-2}).$$ (2.55)

6. Desired distribution of retained earnings:

$$DA_{ft}^D = (C_{ft}^D, D_{ft}^D, T_{ft}^D, G_{ft}^D, N_{ft}^D).$$ (2.59)

7. Desired level of cash (currency) balances:

$$C_{ft}^D = a_5 [P_{ct}X_{ct} + P_{kt}X_{kt}] \qquad (2.61)$$
$$= a_5\ PX.$$

8. Desired level of demand deposits:

$$D_{ft}^D = d_f(PX) + A_6\bar{r}_f. \qquad (2.62)$$

9. Desired level of time deposits:

$$T_{ft}^D = t_f(PX) + A_7\bar{r}_f. \qquad (2.63)$$

10. Desired level of government securities:

$$G_{ft}^D = g_f(PX) + A_8\bar{r}_f. \qquad (2.64)$$

11. Desired level of deposits in intermediaries:

$$N_{ft}^D = n_f(PX) + A_9\bar{r}_f. \qquad (2.65)$$

12. Contribution of firms to public's income:

$$Y_{ft} = PX_t + r_{g_t}G_{ft} + r_{t_t}T_{ft} + r_{n_t}N_{ft} + L_{ft} +$$
$$B_{ft} - \Delta(A_{ft}) - \Sigma L_{ft} - \Sigma F_{ft} - P_{kt}X_{kft}. \qquad (2.71)$$

The Government

1. Tax receipts:

$$T = t\bar{Y}. \qquad (2.72)$$

2. Government spending:

$$T = \bar{r}_g\bar{G} + P_kX_{kg} + P_cX_{cg}. \qquad (2.73)$$

3. Supply and demand for government securities:

$$G^S \equiv G^{Da}. \qquad (2.78)$$

4. Rediscounting:

$$d \equiv d^d(r_d).$$ (2.79)

5. Stock of currency:

$$C_t \equiv C_t^{Da}.$$ (2.81)

6. Rate on government securities:

$$r_{gt} = r_{gt-1} - g(G_{t-1}^D - G_{t-2}^D).$$

The Banking Sector

1. Demand for time deposits:

$$T_t = T_t^D \equiv T_{pt}^S + T_{ft}^S + T_{nt}^S.$$ (2.83)

2. The rate of interest on time deposits:

$$r_t = r_{tt-1} + a(\bar{L}_b - L_{bp}^D - L_{bf}^D).$$ (2.86)

3. Demand for demand deposits:

$$D_t = D_t^D \equiv D_{pt}^S + D_{ft}^S + D_{nt}^S.$$ (2.88)

4. Level of legal reserves:

$$R_t = r_t(D_t + T_t).$$ (2.89)

5. Desired currency balances:

$$C_b = \gamma(D + T).$$ (2.90)

6. Desired level of government securities:

$$G_b = \rho(D + T) + A_{10}\bar{r}_b.$$ (2.91)

7. Desired level of firms' securities:

$$F_b = \mu(D + T) + A_{11}\bar{r}_b.$$ (2.92)

8. Loan supply:

$$\bar{L}_t^S = \pi(D_t + T_t) + A_{12}\bar{r}_b \tag{2.96}$$

$$\bar{L}_{pt}^{Sb} = \ell_p^b \bar{L}_t^S + a_{13}(r_{bpt} - r_{bft}) \tag{2.97}$$

$$\bar{L}_{ft}^{Sb} = \ell_f^b \bar{L}_t^S - a_{13}(r_{bpt} - r_{bft}). \tag{2.98}$$

9. Demand for rediscounting:

$$d_t^d = \bar{L}_{pt}^{Db} + \bar{L}_{ft}^{Db} - (\bar{L}_{pt}^{Sb} + \bar{L}_{ft}^{Sb}) - \frac{d_o}{r_{bpt} - r_{dt}} -$$

$$\frac{d_1}{r_{bft} - r_{dt}} \tag{2.101}$$

$$d_{ot}^d = \bar{L}_{pt}^{Db} - \bar{L}_{pt}^{Sb} - (\bar{L}_{ft}^{Sb} - \bar{L}_{ft}^{Db}) - \frac{d_o}{r_{bpt} - r_{dt}} \tag{2.102}$$

$$d_{lt}^d = \bar{L}_{ft}^{Db} - \bar{L}_{ft}^{Sb} - (\bar{L}_{pt}^{Sb} - \bar{L}_{pt}^{Db}) - \frac{d_1}{r_{bft} - r_{dt}} \tag{2.103}$$

10. Actual amounts lent each sector:

$$L_{pt}^b = \min \left\{ \bar{L}_{pt}^{Db}, \bar{L}_{pt}^{Sb} + (\bar{L}_{ft}^{Sb} - \bar{L}_{ft}^{Db}) + d_{ot}^d \right\} \tag{2.106}$$

$$L_{ft}^b = \min \left\{ \bar{L}_{ft}^{Db}, \bar{L}_{ft}^{Sb} + (\bar{L}_{pt}^{Sb} - \bar{L}_{pt}^{Db}) + d_{lt}^d \right\} \tag{2.107}$$

11. Rates of interest on bank loans:

$$r_{bpt} = r_{bpt-1} + a_p(\bar{L}_{pt-1}^{Db} - \bar{L}_{pt-1}^{Sb}) +$$
$$b_p(r_{pt-1} - r_{npt-1}) \tag{2.108}$$

$$r_{bft} = r_{bft-1} + a_f(\bar{L}_{ft-1}^{Db} - \bar{L}_{ft-1}^{Sb}) +$$
$$b_f(r_{bft-1} - r_{nft-1}). \tag{2.109}$$

12. Contribution to public's income:

$$Y_b^{m+1} = \pi_b^{m+1} - P_{km+1}X_{kbm+1} . \tag{2.122}$$

The Intermediaries

   1. The supply of deposits:

$$N = N^S \equiv N^D \tag{2.123}$$

   2. Supply of loans:

$$\bar{L}_n^S = \ell_n N + A_{14}\bar{r}_n \tag{2.125}$$

$$\bar{L}_{pt}^{Sn} = \ell_p^n L_{nt}^{Sn} + a_{18}(r_{npt} - r_{nft}) \tag{2.130}$$

$$\bar{L}_{ft}^{Sn} = \ell_p^n \bar{L}_{nt}^{Sn} - a_{18}(r_{npt} - r_{nft}). \tag{2.131}$$

   3. Desired level of government securities:

$$G_n^D = g_n N + A_{15}\bar{r}_n. \tag{2.126}$$

   4. Desired level of demand deposits:

$$D_n^D = d_n N + A_{16}\bar{r}_n. \tag{2.127}$$

   5. Desired level of firms' securities:

$$F_n^D = b_n N + A_{17}\bar{r}_n. \tag{2.128}$$

   6. Desired currency balances:

$$C_n^D = c_n N. \tag{2.129}$$

   7. Actual amounts lent:

$$L_{np} = \min \ \left\{ L_{np}^S + (\bar{L}_f^{Sn} - L_f^{Dn}), L_{np}^D \right\} \tag{2.133}$$

$$L_{nf} = \min \ \left\{ L_{nf}^S + (\bar{L}_p^{Sn} - L_p^{Dn}), L_{nf}^S \right\} \tag{2.134}$$

   8. Rates of interest:

$$r_{nft+1} = r_{nft} + a_{19}(L_{nft}^{Sn} - L_{ft}^{Dn}) +$$
$$b_{19}(r_{nft} - r_{bft}) \tag{2.138}$$

$$r_{npt+1} = r_{npt} + a_{20}(L_{np}^S - L_{np}^D) +$$
$$b_{20}(r_{np} - r_{bp}) \tag{2.139}$$

$$r_{nt+1} = r_{nt} + a_{21}(L_n^S - L_{np}^D - L_{nf}^D). \tag{2.140}$$

9. Intermediaries' contribution to public's income:

$$Y_n^t = \pi_n^t - P_{kt}X_{knt}. \tag{2.150}$$

The Public Sector

1. Desired level of demand deposits:

$$D_{pt} = k_1 Y_t + A_{22}\bar{r}_p. \tag{2.151}$$

2. Desired currency balances:

$$C_{pt} = k_2 Y_t + A_{23}\bar{r}_p. \tag{2.152}$$

3. Desired level of time deposits:

$$T_{pt} = k_3 Y_t + A_{24}\bar{r}_p. \tag{2.153}$$

4. Demand for the consumption good:

$$C_{nt} = cY_t + A_{25}\bar{r}_p. \tag{2.154}$$

5. Desired level of government securities:

$$G_{pt} = gY_t + A_{26}\bar{r}_p. \tag{2.155}$$

6. Demand for bank loans:

$$L_{pt}^{Db} = \ell_p^b Y_t + A_{27}\bar{r}_p. \tag{2.156}$$

7. Demand for intermediary loans:

$$L_{pt}^{Dn} = \ell_p^n Y_t + A_{28}\bar{r}_p. \tag{2.157}$$

8. Demand for firms' securities:

$$F_{pt} = f_p Y_t + A_{29} \bar{r}_p. \tag{2.158}$$

9. Demand for deposits in intermediaries:

$$N_{pt} = n_p Y_t + A_{30} \bar{r}_p. \tag{2.159}$$

10. Gross income:

$$\bar{Y}_t = Y_{gt} + Y_{bt} + Y_{nt} + Y_{ft} + r_{gt} G_{pt} + r_{nt} N_{pt} +$$
$$r_{tt} T_{pt} + r_{ft} F_{pt}. \tag{2.160}$$

11. Disposable income:

$$Y_t = (1 - t) \bar{Y}_t. \tag{2.161}$$

3. Solution with a Passive Government

T HE EFFECTS of changes in the variables of the model on the stock of money, and vice versa, will be considered here, under the assumption that the government is essentially passive, that is, the government does not engage in active monetary or fiscal policy. The reserve requirement, r, is fixed at r*; the discount rate is fixed at r_d^*; and the government is a passive supplier-absorber of government securities.

The solution to the model concentrates on two areas: the effects of changes in the variables in the model on the stock of money, and the effects of changes in the money stock on the variables of the model. In the first case the solution is designed to yield the following expressions: $\partial M/\partial r$ for all r, $\partial M/\partial Y$, $\partial M/\partial P$ for all P, $\partial M/\partial X$ for all X, a total of thirteen expressions (M the dependent variable). In the second case, we consider $\partial X/\partial M$ for all X, $\partial Y/\partial M$, $\partial P/\partial M$ for all P, and $\partial r/\partial M$ for all r, thirteen more expressions (M the independent variable). Due to the complexity of the model to be solved it is not in general true that, for example, $\partial M/\partial PX_c = 1/\partial P_c/\partial M$. Thus, different methods of solution will be used in each case in order to avoid making such (possibly) erroneous assumptions.

AN EXPRESSION FOR THE MONEY STOCK

Time deposits and deposits in the intermediaries are not considered part of the stock of money. (These could be easily included in the analysis by simply adding T and N to Equation 3.1.) The stock of money in existence in period t, M_t, is thus simply the sum of all currency holdings and all demand deposits:

$$M_t = C_{pt} + C_{bt} + C_{nt} + C_{ft} + D_{pt} + D_{nt} + D_{ft}. \tag{3.1}$$

Substituting the appropriate expressions from chapter 2 for each of the expressions in 3.1 and simplifying, we obtain

$$M = (a_5 + d_f)(PX) + (d_n + c_n)N + (k_1 + k_2)Y +$$
$$\gamma(D + T) + \bar{r}_p(A_{22} + A_{23}) + \bar{r}_f A_6 + \bar{r}_n A_{16}. \qquad (3.2)$$

(The t subscript has been dropped in 3.2.) Substituting the expressions for N and D + T from chapter 2 yields an expression for M in terms of PX (the value of goods produced), Y (disposable income), the various rates of interest, and the parameters of the model.

$$M = PX(a_5 + d_f + n_f d_n + n_f c_n + \gamma d_f + \gamma t_f + \gamma d_n n_f) +$$
$$Y(d_{np} + c_n n_p + k_1 + k_2 + \gamma d_n n_p + \gamma k_1 + \gamma k_3) +$$
$$\bar{r}_p[(d_n + c_n + \gamma d_n)A_{30} + (1 + \gamma)A_{22} + A_{23} + \gamma A_{24}] +$$
$$\bar{r}_f[(d_n + c_n + \gamma d_n)A_9 + (1 + \gamma)A_6 + \gamma A_7] +$$
$$\bar{r}_n[(1 + \gamma)A_{16}]. \qquad (3.3)$$

Using $C_1, \ldots, C_5$ for the parametric terms in 3.4, we have

$$M = PX\, C_1 + Y\, C_2 + \bar{r}_p C_3 + \bar{r}_f C_4 + \bar{r}_n C_5. \qquad (3.4)$$

This expression for the money stock plays a key role in the solution of the model.

SOLUTION WITH M AS THE DEPENDENT VARIABLE

The solution in this case begins with differentiation of Equation 3.4. This yields the following equations:

$$\frac{\partial M}{\partial r_f} = C_1 \left[\frac{\partial P_c}{\partial r_f} X_c + \frac{\partial X_c}{\partial r_f} P_c + \frac{\partial P_k}{\partial r_f} X_k + \frac{\partial X_k}{\partial r_f} P_k \right] +$$

$$C_2 \frac{\partial Y}{\partial r_f} + C_3 \frac{\partial \bar{r}_f}{\partial r_f} + C_4 \frac{\partial \bar{r}_p}{\partial r_f} + C_5 \frac{\partial \bar{r}_n}{\partial r_f} \qquad (3.5)^1$$

1. Equations 3.6–3.11 have not been reproduced because they follow in sequence from Equation 3.5.

.

.

.

$$\frac{\partial M}{\partial r_{np}} = C_1 \left[\frac{\partial P_c}{\partial r_{np}} X_c + \frac{\partial X_c}{\partial r_{np}} P_c + \frac{\partial P_k}{\partial r_{np}} X_k + \frac{\partial X_k}{\partial r_{np}} P_k \right] +$$

$$C_2 \frac{\partial Y}{\partial r_{np}} + C_3 \frac{\partial \overline{r}_f}{\partial r_{np}} + C_4 \frac{\partial \overline{r}_p}{\partial r_{np}} + C_5 \frac{\partial \overline{r}_n}{\partial r_{np}}, \tag{3.12}$$

where the $\partial \overline{r}_{f,p,n} / \partial r$'s are vectors of partial derivatives; for example,

$$\frac{\partial \overline{r}_n}{\partial r_f} = \left(1, \frac{\partial r_g}{\partial r_f}, \frac{\partial r_n}{\partial r_f}, \frac{\partial r_t}{\partial r_f}, 0, 0, \frac{\partial r_{nf}}{\partial r_f}, \frac{\partial r_{np}}{\partial r_f} \right).$$

$$\frac{\partial M}{\partial Y} = C_1 \left[\frac{\partial P_c}{\partial Y} X_c + \frac{\partial X_c}{\partial Y} P_c + \frac{\partial P_k}{\partial Y} X_k + \frac{\partial X_k}{\partial Y} P_k \right] +$$

$$C_2 + C_3 \frac{\partial \overline{r}_f}{\partial Y} + C_4 \frac{\partial \overline{r}_p}{\partial Y} + C_5 \frac{\partial \overline{r}_n}{\partial Y} \tag{3.13}$$

$$\frac{\partial M}{\partial P_c} = C_1 \left[X_c + \frac{\partial X_c}{\partial P_c} P_c + \frac{\partial P_k}{\partial P_c} X_k + \frac{\partial X_k}{\partial P_c} P_k \right] +$$

$$C_2 \frac{\partial Y}{\partial P_c} + C_3 \frac{\partial \overline{r}_f}{\partial P_c} + C_4 \frac{\partial \overline{r}_p}{\partial P_c} + C_5 \frac{\partial \overline{r}_n}{\partial P_c} \tag{3.14}$$

$$\frac{\partial M}{\partial P_k} = \cdot \quad \cdot \quad \cdot \quad \cdot \quad \cdot \quad \cdot \quad \cdot \quad \cdot \tag{3.15}$$

$$\frac{\partial M}{\partial X_c} = C_1 \left[P_c + \frac{\partial P_c}{\partial X_c} X_c + \frac{\partial P_k}{\partial X_c} X_k + \frac{\partial X_k}{\partial X_c} P_k \right] +$$

$$C_2 \frac{\partial Y}{\partial X_c} + C_3 \frac{\partial \overline{r}_f}{\partial X_c} + C_4 \frac{\partial \overline{r}_p}{\partial X_c} + C_5 \frac{\partial \overline{r}_n}{\partial X_c} \tag{3.16}$$

$$\frac{\partial M}{\partial X_k} = \cdot \quad \cdot \quad \cdot \quad \cdot \quad \cdot \quad \cdot \quad \cdot \quad \cdot \qquad (3.17)$$

This system of thirteen equations contains the following unknowns:

1. $\dfrac{\partial r_i}{\partial r_j}$ ∀ i, j (=1 when i = j)   (56 unknowns);

2. $\dfrac{\partial Y}{\partial r}$ ∀ r   (8 unknowns);

3. $\dfrac{\partial P}{\partial r}$ ∀ P, r   (4 unknowns);

4. $\dfrac{\partial X}{\partial r}$ ∀ X, r   (4 unknowns);

5. $\dfrac{\partial P}{\partial Y}$ ∀ P   (2 unknowns);

6. $\dfrac{\partial X}{\partial Y}$ ∀ X   (2 unknowns);

7. $\dfrac{\partial r}{\partial Y}$ ∀ r   (8 unknowns);

8. $\dfrac{\partial X}{\partial P}$ ∀ X, P   (4 unknowns);

9. $\dfrac{\partial P_i}{\partial P_j}$ i ≠ j   (2 unknowns);

10. $\dfrac{\partial Y}{\partial P}$ ∀ P   (2 unknowns);

11. $\dfrac{\partial r}{\partial P}$ ∀ r, P   (16 unknowns);

12. $\dfrac{\partial X_i}{\partial X_j}$ i ≠ j   (2 unknowns);

13. $\dfrac{\partial P}{\partial X}$ $\forall$ P, X (4 unknowns);

14. $\dfrac{\partial Y}{\partial X}$ $\forall$ X (2 unknowns);

15. $\dfrac{\partial r}{\partial X}$ $\forall$ r, X (16 unknowns).

Expressing the unknowns in (1) above in matrix form we have

$$
\begin{bmatrix}
1 & r_{gf} & r_{nf} & r_{tf} & r_{bff} & r_{bpf} & r_{nff} & r_{npf} \\
r_{fg} & 1 & r_{ng} & r_{tg} & r_{bfg} & r_{npg} & r_{nfg} & r_{npg} \\
r_{nf} & r_{gn} & 1 & r_{tn} & r_{bfn} & r_{bpn} & r_{nfn} & r_{npn} \\
r_{ft} & r_{gt} & r_{nt} & 1 & r_{bft} & r_{bpt} & r_{nft} & r_{npt} \\
r_{fbf} & r_{gbf} & r_{nbf} & r_{tbf} & 1 & r_{bpbf} & r_{nfbf} & r_{npbf} \\
r_{fbp} & r_{gbp} & r_{nbp} & r_{tbp} & r_{bfbp} & 1 & r_{nfbp} & r_{npbp} \\
r_{fnf} & r_{gnf} & r_{nnf} & r_{tnf} & r_{bfnf} & r_{bpnf} & 1 & r_{npnf} \\
r_{fnp} & r_{gnp} & r_{nnp} & r_{tnp} & r_{bfnp} & r_{bpnp} & r_{nfnp} & 1
\end{bmatrix}
$$

where $r_{ij} = \partial r_i / \partial r_j$. For example, $r_{bfnp} = \partial r_{bf} / \partial r_{np}$. The series of 1's down the principal diagonal are the r_{ii}.

Below are the relations describing how the various rates of interest are assumed to change over time:

$$r_{nft} = r_{nft-1} + a_{19}(L_{nft-1}^{Sn} - L_{ft}^{Dn}) + b_{19}$$
$$(r_{nft-1} - r_{bft-1}) \tag{2.138}$$

$$r_{npt} = r_{npt-1} + a_{20}(L_{npt-1}^{S} - L_{npt-1}^{D}) + b_{20}$$
$$(r_{npt-1} - r_{bpt-1}) \tag{2.139}$$

$$r_{nt} = r_{nt-1} + a_{21}(L_n^{S} - L_{np}^{D} - L_{nf}^{D}) \tag{2.140}$$

$$r_t = r_{tt-1} + a(\bar{L}_b - L_{bp}^{D} - L_{bf}^{D}) \tag{2.86}$$

$$r_{bpt} = r_{bpt-1} + a_p(\overline{L}_{pt-1}^{Db} - \overline{L}_{pt-1}^{Sb}) + b_p$$
$$(r_{bpt-1} - r_{npt-1}) \tag{2.108}$$

$$r_{bft} = r_{bft-1} + a_f(\overline{L}_{ft-1}^{Db} - \overline{L}_{ft-1}^{Sb}) + b_f$$
$$(r_{bft-1} - r_{nft-1}) \tag{2.109}$$

$$r_f = r_{ft-1} + f(B_{ft-1}^S - B_{ft-1}^D) \tag{3.18}$$

$$r_g = r_{gt-1} - g(G_{t-1}^S - G_{t-1}^D). \tag{3.19}$$

Differentiation of these relations with respect to the r's reveals that the terms in the "interest-interaction" matrix depend on the effects of changes in the r's on the quantity demanded and quantity supplied of loans and of firms' securities; the quantity demanded of government securities; on institutional linkages between various rates (such as between the rates charged by different sectors on loans to the public and the rates charged by the banks on loans to the various sectors); and on the sensitivity of rates on deposits to either an excess supply or demand for loans in the previous period (the sizes of a_{19}, a_{20}, a_{21}, a, a_p, etc.). Differentiation of this system would yield a system of fifty-six equations in the fifty-six interest-interaction terms and $\partial Y/\partial r$ ∀ r, $\partial X/\partial r$ ∀ r, X, and $\partial P/\partial r$ ∀ r, P. Differentiation with respect to Y will yield expressions for the $\partial r/\partial Y$. Multiplying this result by $\partial Y/\partial P$ ∀ P will yield expressions for $\partial r/\partial P$ ∀ P, while multiplying the original result by $\partial Y/\partial X$ ∀ X gives $\partial r/\partial X$ ∀ r, X. This will be discussed later.

The expressions for $\partial Y/\partial r$, $\partial Y/\partial P$, and $\partial Y/\partial X$ ∀ r can be obtained by differentiating the expressions for Y,

$$Y = PX + \pi_b + \pi_n + r_g G + r_t T_p + r_n N_p + r_f B_{fp} -$$
$$r_{bf} L_{bf} - r_{nf} L_{nf}$$

with respect to each of the r's, P's, and X's.

The expressions for $\partial P/\partial r$, $\partial X/\partial r$, $\partial X/\partial Y$, $\partial P/\partial Y$, and $\partial P_i/\partial P_j$ can be obtained from the implicit supply and demand functions for X_c and X_k. These are

$$S_k = s_k(P_k, P_c, \bar{r}) \tag{3.20}$$

$$D_k = d_k(P_k, P_c, \bar{r}) \tag{3.21}$$

$$S_c = s_c(P_k, P_c, \bar{r}, Y) \tag{3.22}$$

$$D_c = d_c(P_k, P_c, \bar{r}, Y). \tag{3.23}$$

The general technique is to differentiate both the supply and demand equations for one good with respect to the r's (or Y) and then impose the equilibrium condition that $S_x = D_x$. For example, differentiating 3.20 and 3.21 with respect to r_f yields

$$\frac{\partial S_k}{\partial r_f} = \frac{\partial s_k}{\partial P_k} \frac{\partial P_k}{\partial r_f} + \frac{\partial s_k}{\partial P_c} \frac{\partial P_c}{\partial r_f} + \frac{\partial s_k}{\partial \bar{r}} \frac{\partial \bar{r}}{\partial r_f}$$

$$\frac{\partial D_k}{\partial r_f} = \frac{\partial d_k}{\partial P_k} \frac{\partial P_k}{\partial r_f} + \frac{\partial d_k}{\partial P_c} \frac{\partial P_c}{\partial r_f} + \frac{\partial d_k}{\partial \bar{r}} \frac{\partial \bar{r}}{\partial r_f}.$$

At equilibrium $\dfrac{\partial S_k}{\partial r_f} dr_f = \dfrac{\partial D_k}{\partial r_f} dr_f$, so that

$$\left(\frac{\partial s_k}{\partial P_k} \frac{\partial P_k}{\partial r_f} + \frac{\partial s_k}{\partial P_c} \frac{\partial P_c}{\partial r_f} + \frac{\partial s_k}{\partial \bar{r}} \frac{\partial \bar{r}}{\partial r_f} \right) dr_f =$$

$$\left(\frac{\partial d_k}{\partial P_k} \frac{\partial P_k}{\partial r_f} + \frac{\partial d_k}{\partial P_c} \frac{\partial P_c}{\partial r_f} + \frac{\partial d_k}{\partial \bar{r}} \frac{\partial \bar{r}}{\partial r_f} \right) dr_f. \tag{3.24}$$

Canceling dr_f from both sides, and simplifying,

$$\frac{\partial P_k}{\partial r_f} = \frac{\dfrac{\partial P_c}{\partial r_f} \left(\dfrac{\partial d_k}{\partial P_c} - \dfrac{\partial s_k}{\partial P_c} \right) + \dfrac{\partial \bar{r}}{\partial r_f} \left(\dfrac{\partial d_k}{\partial \bar{r}} - \dfrac{\partial s_k}{\partial \bar{r}} \right)}{\dfrac{\partial s_k}{\partial P_k} - \dfrac{\partial d_k}{\partial P_k}}. \tag{3.25}$$

Differentiating 3.22 and 3.23 with respect to r_f and following the same procedure,

$$\frac{\partial P_c}{\partial r_f} = \frac{\frac{\partial P_k}{\partial r_f}\left(\frac{\partial d_c}{\partial P_k} - \frac{\partial s_c}{\partial P_k}\right) + \frac{\partial \bar{r}}{\partial r_f}\left(\frac{\partial d_c}{\partial \bar{r}} - \frac{\partial s_k}{\partial \bar{r}}\right)}{\frac{\partial s_c}{\partial P_c} - \frac{\partial d_c}{\partial P_c}}.$$ (3.26)

Equations 3.25 and 3.26 form a system of two equations that can be solved simultaneously for the unknowns $\partial P_k/\partial r_f$ and $\partial P_c/\partial r_f$. Repeating this procedure will yield $\partial P/\partial r$ $\forall$ P, r.

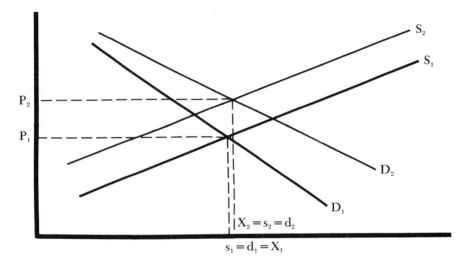

Fig. 14. Changes in P and X

The same system (3.20 to 3.23) is used to solve for $\partial X/\partial r$. We start with an equilibrium situation where s_1 and d_1 (the K and C subscripts) have been omitted since the technique is the same for both. See Figure 14. We then imagine a change in one of the elements of r that results in a shift in both the demand and supply curves to D_2 and S_2. This results in changes in both X and P. The expression for $\partial P/\partial X$ was developed in the last paragraph. The equilibrium change in X is obtained in this manner:

$$X_1 = d_k(P_1, P_c, \bar{r}) = s_k(P_1, P_c, \bar{r})$$

$$X_2 = d_k(P_1 + \frac{\partial P}{\partial r}\,dr, P_c + \frac{\partial P_c}{\partial r}\,dr, \bar{r} + \frac{\partial \bar{r}}{\partial r}\,dr)$$

$$= s_k(P_1 + \frac{\partial P}{\partial r} dr, \; P_c + \frac{\partial P_c}{\partial r} dr, \; \bar{r} + \frac{\partial \bar{r}}{\partial r} dr).$$

The change in X, given the change in r, is simply $X_2 - X_1$ or

$$d_k(P_1 + \frac{\partial P}{\partial r} dr, \; P_c + \frac{\partial P_c}{\partial r} dr, \; \bar{r} + \frac{\partial \bar{r}}{\partial r} dr) - d_k(P_1, P_c, \bar{r})$$

$$\frac{\Delta X}{\Delta r} = d_k \left(\frac{\partial P}{\partial r} dr, \; \frac{\partial P_c}{\partial r} dr, \; \frac{\partial \bar{r}}{\partial r} dr \right) = s_k \left(\frac{\partial P}{\partial r} dr, \; \frac{\partial P_c}{\partial r} dr, \; \frac{\partial \bar{r}}{\partial r} dr \right).$$

$$(3.27)$$

In the limit as $\Delta r \to 0$, $\Delta X / \Delta r \to \partial X / \partial r$ which is still given by either expression in 3.27. Repetition of this process yields $\partial X / \partial r$ for all X and r.

The expressions for $\partial P / \partial Y$ and $\partial X / \partial Y$ are obtained in an analogous manner which will not be repeated here. The same technique is also used to obtain expressions for $\partial P_i / \partial P_j$.

The expressions for $\partial X_k / \partial X_c$ and $\partial X_c / \partial X_k$ can be obtained directly from the transformation function. These relations obtained by differentiating the transformation function hold only in a situation of full employment. At less than full employment, these rates of change may approach $+ \infty$ if the economy begins to utilize previously unused capital and/or labor.

The expressions for $\partial X_i / \partial P_i$ are obtained in a manner analogous to the above by differentiation of the supply and demand functions and the imposition of the equilibrium condition that quantity supplied equals quantity demanded.

Before commenting further on the solution with M as the dependent variable, we will consider the solution with M as the independent variable because of the close similarity of the technique in this case and that used above.

SOLUTION WITH M AS THE INDEPENDENT VARIABLE

The rates of change we wish to develop here measure the effects of changes in the stock of money on the key variables in the model. Thus, we are interested in obtaining expressions for $\partial X_k / \partial M$, $\partial X_c / \partial M$, $\partial Y / \partial M$, $\partial P_c / \partial M$, $\partial P_k / \partial M$, and $\partial r / \partial M \; \forall \; r$. As indicated earlier, it is not sufficient to assume that these rates of change are simply the inverses of those obtained earlier due to the complexity of the model. They may be, but in general it cannot be expected that they will be.

To obtain expressions for $\partial P/\partial M$ and $\partial X/\partial M$, the implicit supply and demand functions 3.20 to 3.23 are again used. Differentiation of 3.20 and 3.21 with respect to M yields

$$\frac{\partial S_k}{\partial M} = \frac{\partial s_k}{\partial P_k}\frac{\partial P_k}{\partial M} + \frac{\partial s_k}{\partial P_c}\frac{\partial P_c}{\partial M} + \frac{\partial s_k}{\partial \bar{r}}\frac{\partial \bar{r}}{\partial M} . \qquad (3.28)$$

$$\frac{\partial D_k}{\partial M} = \frac{\partial d_k}{\partial P_k}\frac{\partial P_k}{\partial M} + \frac{\partial d_k}{\partial P_c}\frac{\partial P_c}{\partial M} + \frac{\partial d_k}{\partial \bar{r}}\frac{\partial \bar{r}}{\partial M} . \qquad (3.29)$$

Again, for equilibrium, $\partial S_k/\partial M \ dM = \partial D_k/\partial M \ dM$ so that, by equating 3.28 and 3.29 and simplifying, we obtain

$$\frac{\partial P_k}{\partial M} = \frac{\dfrac{\partial P_c}{\partial M}\left(\dfrac{\partial d_k}{\partial P_c} - \dfrac{\partial s_k}{\partial P_c}\right) + \dfrac{\partial \bar{r}}{\partial M}\left(\dfrac{\partial d_k}{\partial \bar{r}} - \dfrac{\partial s_k}{\partial \bar{r}}\right)}{\dfrac{\partial s_k}{\partial P_k} + \dfrac{\partial d_k}{\partial P_k}} . \qquad (3.30)$$

Proceeding in the same manner we obtain the expression for $\partial P_c/\partial M$. This system can then be solved for $\partial P_c/\partial M$ and $\partial P_k/\partial M$ in terms of the parameters of the supply and demand functions and $\partial \bar{r}/\partial M$.

The expressions for $\partial X/\partial M$ we obtained in the same manner in which those for $\partial X/\partial r$ were obtained in the section on solution with M as the dependent variable. Thus,

$$\frac{\partial X_k}{\partial M} = d_k \left(\frac{\partial P_k}{\partial M}dM, \ \frac{\partial P_c}{\partial M}dM, \ \frac{\partial \bar{r}}{\partial M}dM\right)$$

$$= s_k \left(\frac{\partial P_k}{\partial M}dM, \ \frac{\partial P_c}{\partial M}dM, \ \frac{\partial \bar{r}}{\partial M}dM\right) \qquad (3.31)$$

and similarly for $\partial X_c/\partial M$.

The expressions for $\partial r/\partial M$ are obtained from the relations in the section on solution with M as the dependent variable, describing the determination of various rates of interest.

Each of these relations is differentiated with respect to M. In general, the expressions for $\partial r/\partial M$ depend upon the effects of changes in the money stock on the demand and supply of loans, firms' securities, and government securities. These effects are, in turn, primarily dependent upon the influences of changes in the money stock on the various rates of interest. This procedure yields a system of eight relations in $\partial r/\partial M$ which can then be solved simultaneously, yielding solutions in terms of $\partial Y/\partial M$, $\partial X/\partial M$, and $\partial P/\partial M$.

The expression for $\partial Y/\partial M$ is obtained by differentiating the expression for Y,

$$Y = PX + \pi b + \pi_n + r_g G + r_t T_p + r_n N_p + r_f B_{fp} - r_{bf}L_{bf} - r_{nf}L_{nf},$$

with respect to M, yielding

$$\frac{\partial Y}{\partial M} = \frac{\partial X_c}{\partial M} P_c + \frac{\partial P_c}{\partial M} X_c + \frac{\partial X_k}{\partial M} P_k + \frac{\partial P_k}{\partial M} X_k + \frac{\partial \pi_b}{\partial M} +$$

$$\frac{\partial \pi_n}{\partial M} + r_g \frac{\partial G_p}{\partial M} + \frac{\partial r_g}{\partial M} G_p + \frac{\partial r_t}{\partial M} T_p + \frac{\partial r_p}{\partial M} r_t + \frac{\partial r_n}{\partial M} N_p +$$

$$\frac{\partial N_p}{\partial M} r_n + \frac{\partial r_f}{\partial M} B_{fp} + \frac{\partial B_{fp}}{\partial M} r_f - (\frac{\partial r_{bf}}{\partial M} L_{bf} + \frac{\partial L_{bf}}{\partial M} r_{bf} +$$

$$\frac{\partial r_{nf}}{\partial M} L_{nf} + \frac{\partial L_{nf}}{\partial M} r_{nf}) \tag{3.32}$$

where $\dfrac{\partial \pi_b}{\partial M} = f(\dfrac{\partial Y}{\partial M}, \dfrac{\partial L_b}{\partial M})$, $\dfrac{\partial \bar{r}}{\partial M}$, $\dfrac{\partial \pi_n}{\partial M} = f_1(\dfrac{\partial Y}{\partial M}, \dfrac{\partial L_n}{\partial M}, \dfrac{\partial \bar{r}}{\partial M})$,

$\dfrac{\partial G_p}{\partial M} = f_3(\dfrac{\partial Y}{\partial M}, \dfrac{\partial \bar{r}}{\partial M})$, $\dfrac{\partial T_p}{\partial M} = f_4(\dfrac{\partial Y}{\partial M}, \dfrac{\partial \bar{r}}{\partial M})$, $\dfrac{\partial N_p}{\partial M} = f_5(\dfrac{\partial Y}{\partial M}, \dfrac{\partial \bar{r}}{\partial M})$,

$\dfrac{\partial B_{fp}}{\partial M} = f_6(\dfrac{\partial Y}{\partial M}, \dfrac{\partial \bar{r}}{\partial M})$, $\dfrac{\partial L_{bf}}{\partial M} = f_7(\dfrac{\partial PX}{\partial M}, \dfrac{\partial L_D^S}{\partial M}, \dfrac{\partial \bar{r}}{\partial M})$, and

$\dfrac{\partial L_{nf}}{\partial M} = f_8(\dfrac{\partial PX}{\partial M}, \dfrac{\partial L_n^S}{\partial M}, \dfrac{\partial \bar{r}}{\partial M})$.

The "Solution"

The preceding two sections together yield a system of simultaneous equations which could be solved yielding expressions for $\partial - /\partial M$ and $\partial M/\partial -$ (where $-$ represents the variables of interest) in terms of the parameters (the elements of A_i, etc.) alone. No attempt has been made to push the solution to this level. The size and complexity of the resulting expressions would obscure rather than illuminate their economic meaning and significance. Consequently, we will continue to express these relations in terms of partial derivatives, indicating when necessary what variables they depend on. This procedure increases the ease with which the results can be interpreted.

The key results from the previous sections are reproduced here.

$$
\frac{\partial M}{\partial r_f} = C_1 \left[\frac{\partial P_c}{\partial r_f} X_c + \frac{\partial X_c}{\partial r_f} P_c + \frac{\partial P_k}{\partial r_f} X_k + \frac{\partial X_k}{\partial r_f} P_k \right] +
$$

$$
C_2 \frac{\partial Y}{\partial r_f} + C_3 \frac{\partial \bar{r}_f}{\partial r_f} + C_4 \frac{\partial \bar{r}_p}{\partial r_f} + C_5 \frac{\partial \bar{r}_n}{\partial r_f} \tag{3.5}
$$

$$
\frac{\partial M}{\partial r_g} = C_1 \left[\frac{\partial P_c}{\partial r_g} X_c + \frac{\partial X_c}{\partial r_g} P_c + \frac{\partial P_k}{\partial r_g} X_k + \frac{\partial X_k}{\partial r_g} P_k \right] +
$$

$$
C_2 \frac{\partial Y}{\partial r_g} + C_3 \frac{\partial \bar{r}_f}{\partial r_g} + C_4 \frac{\partial \bar{r}_p}{\partial r_g} + C_5 \frac{\partial \bar{r}_n}{\partial r_g} \tag{3.6}
$$

$$
\frac{\partial M}{\partial r_n} = C_1 \left[\frac{\partial P_c}{\partial r_n} X_c + \frac{\partial X_c}{\partial r_n} P_c + \frac{\partial P_k}{\partial r_n} X_k + \frac{\partial X_k}{\partial r_n} P_k \right] +
$$

$$
C_2 \frac{\partial Y}{\partial r_n} + C_3 \frac{\partial \bar{r}_f}{\partial r_n} + C_4 \frac{\partial \bar{r}_p}{\partial r_n} + C_5 \frac{\partial \bar{r}_n}{\partial r_n} \tag{3.7}
$$

$$
\frac{\partial M}{\partial r_t} = C_1 \left[\frac{\partial P_c}{\partial r_t} X_c + \frac{\partial X_c}{\partial r_t} P_c + \frac{\partial P_k}{\partial r_t} X_k + \frac{\partial X_k}{\partial r_t} P_k \right] +
$$

$$
C_2 \frac{\partial Y}{\partial r_t} + C_3 \frac{\partial \bar{r}_f}{\partial r_t} + C_4 \frac{\partial \bar{r}_p}{\partial r_t} + C_5 \frac{\partial \bar{r}_n}{\partial r_t} \tag{3.8}
$$

$$\frac{\partial M}{\partial r_{bf}} = C_1 \left[\frac{\partial P_c}{\partial r_{bf}} X_c + \frac{\partial X_c}{\partial r_{bf}} P_c + \frac{\partial P_k}{\partial r_{bf}} X_k + \frac{\partial X_k}{\partial r_{bf}} P_k \right] +$$

$$C_2 \frac{\partial Y}{\partial r_{bf}} + C_3 \frac{\partial \bar{r}_f}{\partial r_{bf}} + C_4 \frac{\partial \bar{r}_p}{\partial r_{bf}} + C_5 \frac{\partial \bar{r}_n}{\partial r_{bf}} \qquad (3.9)$$

$$\frac{\partial M}{\partial r_{bp}} = C_1 \left[\frac{\partial P_c}{\partial r_{bp}} X_c + \frac{\partial X_c}{\partial r_{bp}} P_c + \frac{\partial P_k}{\partial r_{bp}} X_k + \frac{\partial X_k}{\partial r_{bp}} P_k \right] +$$

$$C_2 \frac{\partial Y}{\partial r_{bp}} + C_3 \frac{\partial \bar{r}_f}{\partial r_{bp}} + C_4 \frac{\partial \bar{r}_p}{\partial r_{bp}} + C_5 \frac{\partial \bar{r}_n}{\partial r_{bp}} \qquad (3.10)$$

$$\frac{\partial M}{\partial r_{nf}} = C_1 \left[\frac{\partial P_c}{\partial r_{nf}} X_c + \frac{\partial X_c}{\partial r_{nf}} P_c + \frac{\partial P_k}{\partial r_{nf}} X_k + \frac{\partial X_k}{\partial r_{nf}} P_k \right] +$$

$$C_2 \frac{\partial Y}{\partial r_{nf}} + C_3 \frac{\partial \bar{r}_f}{\partial r_{nf}} + C_4 \frac{\partial \bar{r}_p}{\partial r_{nf}} + C_5 \frac{\partial \bar{r}_n}{\partial r_{nf}} \qquad (3.11)$$

$$\frac{\partial M}{\partial r_{np}} = C_1 \left[\frac{\partial P_c}{\partial r_{np}} X_c + \frac{\partial X_c}{\partial r_{np}} P_c + \frac{\partial P_k}{\partial r_{np}} X_k + \frac{\partial X_k}{\partial r_{np}} P_k \right] +$$

$$C_2 \frac{\partial Y}{\partial r_{np}} + C_3 \frac{\partial \bar{r}_f}{\partial r_{np}} + C_4 \frac{\partial \bar{r}_p}{\partial r_{np}} + C_5 \frac{\partial \bar{r}_n}{\partial r_{np}} \qquad (3.12)$$

$$\frac{\partial M}{\partial Y} = C_1 \left[\frac{\partial P_c}{\partial Y} X_c + \frac{\partial X_c}{\partial Y} P_c + \frac{\partial P_k}{\partial Y} X_k + \frac{\partial X_k}{\partial Y} P_k \right] +$$

$$C_2 + C_3 \frac{\partial \bar{r}_f}{\partial Y} + C_4 \frac{\partial \bar{r}_p}{\partial Y} + C_5 \frac{\partial \bar{r}_n}{\partial Y} \qquad (3.13)$$

$$\frac{\partial M}{\partial P_c} = C_1 \left[X_c + \frac{\partial X_c}{\partial P_c} P_c + \frac{\partial P_k}{\partial P_c} X_k + \frac{\partial X_k}{\partial P_c} P_k \right] +$$

$$C_2 \frac{\partial Y}{\partial P_c} + C_3 \frac{\partial \bar{r}_f}{\partial P_c} + C_4 \frac{\partial \bar{r}_p}{\partial P_c} + C_5 \frac{\partial \bar{r}_n}{\partial P_c} \qquad (3.14)$$

$$\frac{\partial M}{\partial P_k} = C_1 \left[\frac{\partial P_c}{\partial P_k} X_c + \frac{\partial X_c}{\partial P_k} P_c + X_k + \frac{\partial X_k}{\partial P_k} P_k \right] +$$

$$C_2 \frac{\partial Y}{\partial P_k} + C_3 \frac{\partial \bar{r}_f}{\partial P_k} + C_4 \frac{\partial \bar{r}_p}{\partial P_k} + C_5 \frac{\partial \bar{r}_n}{\partial P_k} \qquad (3.15)$$

$$\frac{\partial M}{\partial X_c} = C_1 \left[\frac{\partial P_c}{\partial X_c} X_c + \frac{\partial P_k}{\partial X_c} X_k + \frac{\partial X_k}{\partial X_c} P_k \right] +$$

$$C_2 \frac{\partial Y}{\partial X_c} + C_3 \frac{\partial \bar{r}_f}{\partial X_c} + C_4 \frac{\partial \bar{r}_p}{\partial X_c} + C_5 \frac{\partial \bar{r}_n}{\partial X_c} \qquad (3.16)$$

$$\frac{\partial M}{\partial X_k} = C_1 \left[\frac{\partial P_c}{\partial X_k} X_c + \frac{\partial X_c}{\partial X_k} P_c + \frac{\partial P_k}{\partial X_k} X_k + P_k \right] +$$

$$C_2 \frac{\partial Y}{\partial X_k} + C_3 \frac{\partial \bar{r}_f}{\partial X_k} + C_4 \frac{\partial \bar{r}_p}{\partial X_k} + C_5 \frac{\partial \bar{r}_n}{\partial X_k} \qquad (3.17)$$

$$\frac{\partial P_k}{\partial M} = \frac{\dfrac{\partial P_c}{\partial M} \left(\dfrac{\partial d_k}{\partial P_c} - \dfrac{\partial s_k}{\partial P_c} \right) + \dfrac{\partial \bar{r}}{\partial M} \left(\dfrac{\partial d_k}{\partial \bar{r}} - \dfrac{\partial s_k}{\partial \bar{r}} \right)}{\dfrac{\partial s_k}{\partial P_k} - \dfrac{\partial d_k}{\partial P_k}} \qquad (3.30)$$

$$\frac{\partial P_c}{\partial M} = \frac{\dfrac{\partial P_k}{\partial M} \left(\dfrac{\partial d_c}{\partial P_k} - \dfrac{\partial s_c}{\partial P_k} \right) + \dfrac{\partial \bar{r}}{\partial M} \left(\dfrac{\partial d_c}{\partial \bar{r}} - \dfrac{\partial s_c}{\partial \bar{r}} \right)}{\dfrac{\partial s_c}{\partial P_c} - \dfrac{\partial d_c}{\partial P_c}} \qquad (3.30a)$$

$$\frac{\partial X_k}{\partial M} = d_k \left(\frac{\partial P_k}{\partial M} dM, \frac{\partial P_c}{\partial M} dM, \frac{\partial \bar{r}}{\partial M} dM \right)$$

$$= s_k \left(\frac{\partial P_k}{\partial M} dM, \frac{\partial P_c}{\partial M} dM, \frac{\partial \bar{r}}{\partial M} dM \right) \qquad (3.31)$$

$$\frac{\partial X_c}{\partial M} = d_c(\frac{\partial P_k}{\partial M}, \frac{\partial P_c}{\partial M}, \frac{\partial \bar{r}}{\partial M}, \frac{\partial Y}{\partial M})$$

$$= s_c(\frac{\partial P_k}{\partial M}, \frac{\partial P_c}{\partial M}, \frac{\partial \bar{r}}{\partial M}, \frac{\partial Y}{\partial M}) \tag{3.31a}$$

$$\frac{\partial Y}{\partial M} = \frac{\partial X_c}{\partial M} P_c + \frac{\partial P_c}{\partial M} X_c + \frac{\partial X_k}{\partial M} P_k + \frac{\partial P_k}{\partial M} X_k +$$

$$\frac{\partial \pi_b}{\partial M} + \frac{\partial \pi_n}{\partial M} + \frac{\partial G_p}{\partial M} r_g + \frac{\partial r_g}{\partial M} G_p + \frac{\partial r_t}{\partial M} T_p +$$

$$\frac{\partial T_p^r}{\partial M} r_t + \frac{\partial r_n}{\partial M} N_p + \frac{\partial N_p}{\partial M} r_n + \frac{\partial r_f}{\partial M} B_{fp} +$$

$$\frac{\partial B_{fp}}{\partial M} r_f - (\frac{\partial r_{bf}}{\partial M} L_{bf} + \frac{\partial L_{bf}}{\partial M} r_{bf} + \frac{\partial r_{nf}}{\partial M} L_{nf} +$$

$$\frac{\partial L_{nf}}{\partial M} r_{nf}) \tag{3.32}$$

It has been indicated previously how the terms on the right-hand side of these relations can be obtained. We now attempt to examine these relations in more detail and to breathe some economic meaning into them.

The expressions $\partial M/\partial r$ depend upon the effects of changes in interest rates on prices, real output, income, and all other interest rates (as well as institutional factors which are represented by the values of the constants C_i). Consider an increase in one rate of interest, r^*. The following statements consider the effects on P from the supply side only. In general, $\partial P/\partial r^* > 0$ when r^* is a cost to the firm (r_{bf}, r_{nf}, and r_f fall into this category). On the other hand, when r^* represents a return to the firm (r_g, r_t, r_n), the effects of an increase in r^* on prices will be less. Conceivably, in some cases, $\partial P/\partial r^*$ for some P and r^* could even be negative. When r^* represents a rate not directly related to the firms (r_{bp} or r_{np}), $\partial P/\partial r^*$ will be very near zero. From the demand side, an increase in r^* represents a potential increase in Y when r^* is r_g, r_n, r_t, or r_f. In these cases, increased Y will also increase the demand for goods and thus tend to increase P. When r^* is either r_{bp} or r_{np}, the net direct effect on Y of an increase in r^* will be zero since increased interest payments will result in increased profit distributions to the owners of the financial sectors. (Indirect effects on Y may be positive or negative depending on the responsiveness of actual amounts lent to changes in r* and the multiplier effects of changes in loans on income.) In general, therefore, we would expect $\partial P/\partial r > 0$.

We would expect $\partial X_k/\partial r^* < 0$ when r* was a cost of investment (r_f, r_{bf}, or r_{nf}), in keeping with standard investment theory. Likewise $\partial X_c/\partial r^* < 0$ would be expected in this case since r* represents a cost to the firm. See Figure 15.

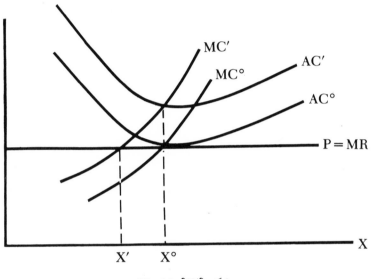

Fig. 15. $\partial X/\partial r < 0$

Here AC' ($> AC°$) is the average cost curve after an increase in r*. Notice that when the demand side is considered as well, it is necessary to point out that increased r* causes an increase in Y which would tend to increase demand and thus X. This effect in general would not be large enough to offset the reduction in X noted earlier, since that reduction itself causes Y to fall, ceteris paribus.

When r* is not directly related to the firm (r_{bp} or r_{np}), we assume $\partial X/\partial r^* = 0$. When r* represents a source of income to the firm (r_g, r_t, r_n), we expect that $\partial X/\partial r^* > 0$ (although these effects are probably small). One straightforward way to think about these effects is to note that increases in these rates may reduce the firms' dependence on financing provided by banks and intermediaries and thus permit greater self-financed expansion.

We have already referred to the effects of changes in r^* on Y as a secondary effect in discussing $\partial P/\partial r^*$ and $\partial X/\partial r^*$. It also enters the expressions for $\partial M/\partial r^*$ directly. The previous discussion will not be repeated here.

The interest-interaction terms $\partial r_i/\partial r_j$ enter the expressions via the last three terms on the right-hand side of 3.5 through 3.13. We hypothesize that $\partial r_i/\partial r_j \geq 0$ for all i, j. This is equivalent to saying that all interest rates tend to move in the same direction. Clearly, the size of the expression will vary, depending on the closeness of the relation between the two rates. For some pairs we would expect this relation to be quite strong (such as $\partial r_{bp}/\partial r_{bf}$), while for others it may be quite weak (such as $\partial r_t/\partial r_{nf}$).

We now turn to a discussion of the constant terms C_1 through C_5.

$$C_1 = (a_5 + d_f + n_f d_n + n_f C_n + \gamma d_f + \gamma t_f + \gamma d_n n_f).$$

Table 3 contains the definitions of these terms and their signs. Clearly, $C_1 > 0$. The value of C_1 tells us by how much the money stock increases, given a one-dollar increase in PX, as a result of the firms' increase in demand for money (a_5 and d_f) and their deposits in banks and intermediaries, which in turn cause these sectors to increase their demands for money ($n_f d_n$—the increase in the intermediaries' demands for demand deposits as a result of firms' increasing their deposits in the intermediaries, etc.). The last term, $\gamma d_n n_f$, is a "third generation" effect—the increase in banks' demand for currency, caused by an increase in intermediaries' demand for deposits, which was in turn a result of an increase in the firms' demand for deposits in the intermediaries.

$$C_2 = (d_n n_p + c_n n_p + k_1 + k_2 + \gamma d_n n_p + \gamma k_1 + \gamma k_3).$$

Table 4 gives the definitions and signs of the terms in C_2 not in C_1. Thus, C_2 is clearly greater than zero. Its interpretation is analogous to that of C_1, except that it measures the effects of an increase in Y on the public's demand for money and the effects of changes in the public's demand on the banks' and intermediaries' demands for money.

$$C_3 = [(d_n + c_n + \gamma d_n)A_{30} + (1 + \gamma)A_{22} + A_{23} + \gamma A_{24}].$$

TABLE 3. Terms of C_1

Term	Sign	Definition
a_5	> 0	Coefficient of PX in firms' demand for currency
d_f	> 0	Coefficient of PX in firms' demand for demand deposits
n_f	> 0	Coefficient of PX in firms' demand for deposits in intermediaries
t_f	> 0	Coefficient of PX in firms' demand for time deposits
γ	> 0	Coefficient of D + T in banks' demand for currency
c_n	> 0	Coefficient of N in intermediaries' demand for currency
d_n	> 0	Coefficient of N in intermediaries' demand for demand deposits

Table 5 gives the definitions and signs of the new terms in C_3.

Thus, with the exception of c_{30} and d_{24}, all terms in A_{30}, A_{22}, A_{23}, and A_{24} are negative since, with the exception of these two terms, they represent the coefficients of rates of interest on competing assets for the public. The interpretation of the actual terms in C_3 is straightforward. For example, $(d_n + c_n + \gamma d_n)A_{30}$ gives the impact of changes in the public's demand for deposits in intermediaries (resulting from a change in some element of $\bar{r}_p$) on the intermediaries' $[(d_n + c_n)A_{30}]$ and the banks' $(d_n A_{30})$ demands for money.

TABLE 4. Terms of C_2

Term	Sign	Definition
n_p	> 0	Coefficient of Y in public's demand for deposits in intermediaries
k_1	> 0	Coefficient of Y in public's demand for currency
k_2	> 0	Coefficient of Y in public's demand for demand deposits
k_3	> 0	Coefficient of Y in public's demand for time deposits

TABLE 5. Terms of C_3

Term	Sign	Definition
A_{30}		Coefficient of $\bar{r}_p$ in public's demand for deposits in intermediaries
a_{30}	< 0	Coefficient of r_f in public's demand for deposits in intermediaries
b_{30}	< 0	Coefficient of r_g in public's demand for deposits in intermediaries
c_{30}	> 0	Coefficient of r_n in public's demand for deposits in intermediaries
d_{30}	< 0	Coefficient of r_t in public's demand for deposits in intermediaries
f_{30}	< 0	Coefficient of r_{bp} in public's demand for deposits in intermediaries
h_{30}	< 0	Coefficient of r_{np} in public's demand for deposits in intermediaries
A_{22}		Coefficient of $\bar{r}_p$ in public's demand for demand deposits
a_{22}	< 0	Coefficient of r_f in public's demand for demand deposits
b_{22}	< 0	Coefficient of r_g in public's demand for demand deposits
c_{22}	< 0	Coefficient of r_n in public's demand for demand deposits
d_{22}	< 0	Coefficient of r_t in public's demand for demand deposits
f_{22}	< 0	Coefficient of r_{bp} in public's demand for demand deposits
h_{22}	< 0	Coefficient of r_{np} in public's demand for demand deposits
A_{23}		Coefficient of $\bar{r}_p$ in public's demand for currency
a_{23}	< 0	Coefficient of r_f in public's demand for currency
b_{23}	< 0	Coefficient of r_g in public's demand for currency
c_{23}	< 0	Coefficient of r_n in public's demand for currency
d_{23}	< 0	Coefficient of r_t in public's demand for currency
f_{23}	< 0	Coefficient of r_{bp} in public's demand for currency
h_{23}	< 0	Coefficient of r_{np} in public's demand for currency

TABLE 5–*Continued*

A_{24}		Coefficient of $\bar{r}_p$ in public's demand for time deposits
a_{24}	< 0	Coefficient of r_f in public's demand for time deposits
b_{24}	< 0	Coefficient of r_g in public's demand for time deposits
c_{24}	< 0	Coefficient of r_n in public's demand for time deposits
d_{24}	> 0	Coefficient of r_t in public's demand for time deposits
f_{24}	< 0	Coefficient of r_{bp} in public's demand for time deposits
h_{24}	< 0	Coefficient of r_{np} in public's demand for time deposits

$$C_4 = [(d_n + c_n + \gamma d_n)A_9 + (1 + \gamma)A_6 + \gamma A_7].$$

The new terms in C_4 are given in Table 6. Once again, all terms but c_9 and d_7 are negative since they represent rates on competing assets for the firms. The interpretation of the actual terms in C_4 is analogous to those of the previous C's. $[(d_n + c_n + \gamma d_n)A_9]$, for example, is the effect of the firms' changed demand for deposits in intermediaries on the intermediaries' and banks' demands for money.

$$C_5 = (1 + \gamma)A_{16}.$$

A_{16} is the coefficient of $\bar{r}_n$ in the intermediaries' demand for demand deposits. Table 7 gives the signs and definitions of the elements of A_{16}.

Thus, C_5 indicates the effects of changes in an element of $\bar{r}_n$ on the intermediaries' demand for demand deposits as well as the secondary effect on the banks' demand for currency.

The preceding discussion and descriptions provide the necessary material to interpret any of the expressions for $\partial M/\partial r^*$ for any r^*.

The expression for $\partial M/\partial Y$ contains the same five constants, C_1 through C_5, described above. Both the derivatives of prices and physical outputs with respect to income will be positive for obvious reasons. The signs of $\partial r^*/\partial Y$ are given in Table 8.

The only sign in Table 8 that can be specified exactly without making further assumptions is that of $\partial r_g/\partial Y$, which will be negative as in-

TABLE 6. Terms of C_4

Term	Sign	Definition
A_9		Coefficient of $\bar{r}_f$ in firms' demand for deposits in intermediaries
a_9	< 0	Coefficient of r_f in firms' demand for deposits in intermediaries
b_9	< 0	Coefficient of r_g in firms' demand for deposits in intermediaries
c_9	> 0	Coefficient of r_n in firms' demand for deposits in intermediaries
d_9	< 0	Coefficient of r_t in firms' demand for deposits in intermediaries
e_9	< 0	Coefficient of r_{bf} in firms' demand for deposits in intermediaries
g_9	< 0	Coefficient of r_{nf} in firms' demand for deposits in intermediaries
A_6		Coefficient of $\bar{r}_f$ in firms' demand for demand deposits
a_6	< 0	Coefficient of r_f in firms' demand for demand deposits
b_6	< 0	Coefficient of r_g in firms' demand for demand deposits
c_6	< 0	Coefficient of r_n in firms' demand for demand deposits
d_6	< 0	Coefficient of r_t in firms' demand for demand deposits
e_6	< 0	Coefficient of r_{bf} in firms' demand for demand deposits
g_6	< 0	Coefficient of r_{nf} in firms' demand for demand deposits
A_7		Coefficient of $\bar{r}_f$ in firms' demand for time deposits
a_7	< 0	Coefficient of r_f in firms' demand for time deposits
b_7	< 0	Coefficient of r_g in firms' demand for time deposits
c_7	< 0	Coefficient of r_n in firms' demand for time deposits
d_7	> 0	Coefficient of r_t in firms' demand for time deposits

TABLE 6—*Continued*

e_7	< 0	Coefficient of r_{bf} in firms' demand for time deposits
g_7	< 0	Coefficient of r_{nf} in firms' demand for time deposits

TABLE 7. Elements of $A_{16}(C_5)$

Term	Sign	Definition
a_{16}	< 0	Coefficient of r_f in intermediaries' demand for demand deposits
b_{16}	< 0	Coefficient of r_g in intermediaries' demand for demand deposits
c_{16}	< 0	Coefficient of r_n in intermediaries' demand for demand deposits
d_{16}	< 0	Coefficient of r_t in intermediaries' demand for demand deposits
g_{16}	< 0	Coefficient of r_{nf} in intermediaries' demand for demand deposits
h_{16}	< 0	Coefficient of r_{np} in intermediaries' demand for demand deposits

TABLE 8. $\dfrac{\partial r^*}{\partial r}$

Term	Sign	Term	Sign
$\dfrac{\partial r_f}{\partial Y}$	$\gtrless 0$	$\dfrac{\partial r_{bf}}{\partial Y}$	$\gtrless 0$
$\dfrac{\partial r_g}{\partial Y}$	< 0	$\dfrac{\partial r_{bp}}{\partial Y}$	$\gtrless 0$
$\dfrac{\partial r_n}{\partial Y}$	$\gtrless 0$	$\dfrac{\partial r_{nf}}{\partial Y}$	$\gtrless 0$
$\dfrac{\partial r_t}{\partial Y}$	$\lessgtr 0$	$\dfrac{\partial r_{np}}{\partial Y}$	$\gtrless 0$

creased demand for government securities will bid their price up and the rate down. The signs of the other terms depend on the relation between the impact of changes in income on the demand for loans and firms' securities and the supply of loans and securities. In a strictly partial equilibrium sense, we can say that if the impact on these demands is greater than on the corresponding supplies, the corresponding partial derivative will be positive. If the impact on the supplies is larger than on the demand, the derivative will be negative. The question of the relative sizes of these effects is not one that can be answered without specifying the actual values of the parameters in the appropriate demand and supply functions. Thus, the answer must be provided either

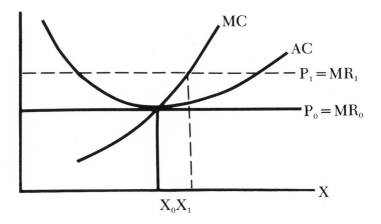

Fig. 16. $\partial X_c/\partial P_c$ and $\partial X_k/\partial P_k$

by assumption on the parameters (which would be only a tentative answer subject to empirical verification) which we have, and will avoid, or by empirical estimation. It could (and will be) argued, however, that, since it is to be expected that increases in income will tend to increase the money stock, if some of the $\partial r/\partial Y$ are in fact negative, they cannot be so negative as to cause the entire expression for $\partial M/\partial Y$ to be negative.

The expressions for $\partial M/\partial P$ also contain C_1 through C_5 as well as the partial derivatives of X_c, X_k, P_c, P_k, Y, and the r's with respect to the P's. The terms $\partial X_c/\partial P_c$ and $\partial X_k/\partial P_k$ are positive under the assumptions of perfect competition. See Figure 16. $\partial Y/\partial P_k$ and $\partial Y/\partial P_c$ are both positive because of the direct relation between PX and Y, and since the terms $\partial X_c/\partial P_c$ and $\partial X_k/\partial P_k$ are (as argued earlier) positive. The terms

$\partial P_c / \partial P_k$ and $\partial P_k / \partial P_c$ are assumed to be positive in deference to the widely observed phenomenon that prices tend to move together. Table 9 lists the remaining terms in the $\partial M / \partial P$ and their signs.

The six terms whose signs are greater than zero simply reflect the fact that as prices increase, so does output, thus increasing the firms' demands for both internal and external financing and thus, ceteris paribus,

TABLE 9. Terms of $\dfrac{\partial M}{\partial P}$

Term	Sign	Term	Sign
$\dfrac{\partial r_f}{\partial P_c}$	> 0	$\dfrac{\partial r_f}{\partial P_k}$	> 0
$\dfrac{\partial r_g}{\partial P_c}$	≈ 0	$\dfrac{\partial r_g}{\partial P_k}$	≈ 0
$\dfrac{\partial r_n}{\partial P_c}$	≈ 0	$\dfrac{\partial r_n}{\partial P_k}$	≈ 0
$\dfrac{\partial r_t}{\partial P_c}$	≈ 0	$\dfrac{\partial r_t}{\partial P_k}$	≈ 0
$\dfrac{\partial r_{bf}}{\partial P_c}$	> 0	$\dfrac{\partial r_{bf}}{\partial P_k}$	> 0
$\dfrac{\partial r_{bn}}{\partial P_c}$	≈ 0	$\dfrac{\partial r_{bn}}{\partial P_k}$	≈ 0
$\dfrac{\partial r_{nf}}{\partial P_c}$	> 0	$\dfrac{\partial r_{nf}}{\partial P_k}$	> 0
$\dfrac{\partial r_{np}}{\partial P_c}$	≈ 0	$\dfrac{\partial r_{np}}{\partial P_k}$	≈ 0

the rates of interest paid on the various types of financing. The notation "≈ 0" is used for the other terms to indicate that they are "nearly" zero, but must be positive since, by our assumption on the interest-interaction terms, all interest rates move together. The causality may, however, not run directly from a change in P_c or P_k to a change in the particular interest rate being considered.

Thus, the terms $\partial M / \partial P_c$ and $\partial M / \partial P_k$ are positive once the assumption (not a very startling one) is granted that $\partial X_{k_{pk}}/\partial P_k > |\ \partial X_k/\partial P_c\ |\ P_k$ and $\partial X_{c_p}/\partial P_c > |\ \partial X_c/\partial P_k\ |\ P_c$.

$\partial M/\partial X_c$ and $\partial M/\partial X_k$ are the last of the key relations in which the five constants C_1 through C_5 enter. With the exception of the terms $\partial X_c/\partial X_k$ and $\partial X_k/\partial X_c$ all terms in these two expressions will also be positive for reasons analogous to those given in the previous argument. At less than full employment these two terms can also be positive (as noted), even though when operating on the transformation curve they must both be negative. Once again, there is no ambiguity about the signs of $\partial M/\partial X_c$ and $\partial M/\partial X_k$ as both will be positive, even with negative $\partial X_i/\partial X_j$.

We turn now to an examination of the expressions in which M appears as the independent variable. The first two of these, $\partial P_k/\partial M$ and $\partial P_c/\partial M$, we have been assured by many, many economists, must be positive. Examination of 3.30 and 3.30a should, we hope, reaffirm the quantity theory. Clearly, the denominators of both of these expressions are positive, since both $\partial d_k/\partial P_k$ and $\partial d_c/\partial P_c$ are negative *if* the demand curves for X_k and X_c are downward sloping. (These derivatives are simply the change in the quantities demanded given a change in price.) What about the numerators? The two terms $\partial s_k/\partial \bar{r}$ and $\partial s_c/\partial \bar{r}$ are negative, since increases in the elements of $\bar{r}$ represent an increase in costs and shift the firms' supply curve (MC) to the left. $\partial d_k/\partial \bar{r}$ and $\partial d_c/\partial \bar{r}$ will both be positive as quantity demanded will increase, given the increase in income caused by increases in the elements of $\bar{r}$. (This effect will be somewhat dampened if increases in $\bar{r}$ reduce loans significantly and thus, indirectly, reduce the amounts of X_k and X_c demanded.) $\partial d_k/\partial P_c$ and $\partial d_c/\partial P_k$ can both be expected to be positive, since increases in the P's will increase income and thus the quantities demanded. So far, all the elements of 3.30 and 3.30a have the proper sign. The only potential source of trouble is in the signs of the elements of $\partial \bar{r}/\partial M$. In general, it is expected that these terms will be negative increases in the money stock, should it tend to reduce rates of interest. Thus, 3.30 and 3.30a will have the "proper" sign (positive) only so long as $\partial P_k/\partial M\ (\partial d_c/\partial P_k - \partial s_c/\partial P_k) > |\ \partial \bar{r}/\partial M\ (\partial d_c/\partial \bar{r} - \partial s_c/\partial \bar{r})\ |$ and likewise in the corresponding expression for $\partial P_k/\partial M$. There seems to be little reason to think this inequality will not be satisfied, since price effects should be more important than interest rate effects on quantities supplied and demanded.

The derivations of the expressions for $\partial X_k/\partial M$ and $\partial X_c/\partial M$ require no further comment since all they amount to is plugging in the equilibrium price change and subtracting from that expression the expression for the original quantity demanded or supplied. The signs of these terms depend on the direction of the effect of changes in M on the demand and supply curves, as well as the location and shape of the initial and final curves. I hypothesize that increases in M cause both demand curves to shift to the right, because of the impact of M on Y. In the event that

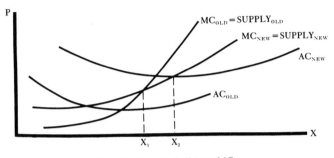

Fig. 17. Effect of dM on MC

the supply curve shifts downward, both $\partial X_k / \partial M$ and $\partial X_c / \partial M$ will be positive. An upward shift in the supply curve is a necessary but not sufficient condition for $\partial X_k / \partial M$ or $\partial X_c / \partial M$ to be negative. For negativity the reduction in supply must be appropriately large. Whether the supply curves shift upward or downward depends on whether, on balance, an increase in M increases or reduces average cost (and thus marginal cost). Interest expenses will tend to fall while the costs of labor and capital tend to increase. On the whole it must be concluded that increases in M tend to increase AC and thus to shift the supply curves to the left for at least a portion of the curve. If changes in M shift not only the position of the AC curve but also affect its shape significantly, the new supply curve (MC curve) may lie above the old curve for other ranges. The argument may be made that increases in M cause such significant increases in demand that firms are induced to build larger plants (perhaps through $\emptyset$, the profits expectations variable, as well as a result of increases in prices) once a situation like Figure 17 consequently results.

In the case illustrated in Figure 17, $\partial X / \partial M$ is clearly positive. In general, we will assume that $\partial X_c / \partial M$ and $\partial X_k / \partial M$ will be positive, although it is clearly not true that in an n-commodity world $\partial X / \partial M \; \forall \; X$ need be positive. Indeed, at full employment in even a two-commodity world, increases in M *cannot* result in changes in the amounts of both commodities produced. This will be dealt with in more detail.

The terms in $\partial Y/\partial M$ are all positive. Clearly $\partial Y/\partial M$ is itself positive. Since Y is defined as money rather than real income, this conclusion should be obvious.

The relations described and discussed above contain the essential information provided by the model on the determination of the stock of money and of the effects of changes in the stock of money on the variables (prices, physical output, income, and interest rates) of the model. These expressions are, of course, rates of change and do not, by themselves, provide us with the actual amount of change in any particular circumstance. This information is derived in the following manner. We know that the money stock is, by definition, the sum of currency outstanding (C) and total demand deposits (D). Thus

$$M = C + D. \tag{3.33}$$

Taking the total differential of this expression yields

$$dM = \frac{\partial C}{\partial \bar{r}}\,d\bar{r} + \frac{\partial C}{\partial Y}\,dY + \frac{\partial C}{\partial P_k}\,dP_k + \frac{\partial C}{\partial P_c}\,dP_c + \frac{\partial C}{\partial X_k}dX_k +$$

$$\frac{\partial C}{\partial X_c}\,dX_c + \frac{\partial D}{\partial \bar{r}}\,d\bar{r} + \frac{\partial D}{\partial Y}\,dY + \frac{\partial D}{\partial P_k}\,dP_k + \frac{\partial D}{\partial P_c}\,dP_c +$$

$$\frac{\partial D}{\partial X_k}\,dX_k + \frac{\partial D}{\partial X_c}\,dX_c. \tag{3.34}$$

Equation 3.34 can be simplified (since D + C = M) to

$$dM = \frac{\partial M}{\partial \bar{r}}\,d\bar{r} + \frac{\partial M}{\partial Y}\,dY + \frac{\partial M}{\partial X_k}\,dX_k + \frac{\partial M}{\partial X_c}\,dX_c +$$

$$\frac{\partial M}{\partial P_k}\,dP_k + \frac{\partial M}{\partial P_c}\,dP_c. \tag{3.35}$$

The partial derivatives on the right-hand side of 3.35 are the terms developed previously. Equation 3.35 provides us with the vehicle to calculate the change in the money stock resulting from a change in one or any combination of the variables $\bar{r}$, Y, X_k, X_c, P_c, or P_k once the size of the change(s) is (are) known.

Equation 3.35 is also a partial differential equation which could be used, given proper boundary conditions, to derive an expression for the money stock.

$$M = \sum_{r=1}^{8} \int \frac{\partial M}{\partial \bar{r}} \, d\bar{r} + \int \frac{\partial M}{\partial Y} \, dY + \int \frac{\partial M}{\partial X_k} \, dX_k +$$

$$\int \frac{\partial M}{\partial X_c} \, dX_c + \int \frac{\partial M}{\partial P_k} \, dP_k + \int \frac{\partial M}{\partial P_c} \, dP_c + K, \qquad (3.36)$$

where K is a composite constant of integration. Since we already have a perfectly good expression for M (see the first part of this chapter), this integration and specification of initial and boundary conditions will not be carried out.

A WORD ON FULL EMPLOYMENT AND EQUILIBRIUM

The questions of the stability, existence, and uniqueness of equilibrium as well as of full employment are beyond the scope of this work. It has been shown that the model can be solved for the value of prices, outputs, income, interest rates, and the money stock, and the inter-relations between these factors have been developed. What we have not shown (or attempted to show) is whether or not this vector of solutions corresponds to a full-employment vector of output. We shall assume that it is possible for our economy to reach full employment without specifying whether or not this occurs (1) without active monetary policy or (2) in conjunction with an "unacceptable" (however defined) rate of increase in prices. In fact, chapter 4 is concerned with the effects and effectiveness of the various tools of monetary policy under two different assumptions about the state of the economy: that the economy is in an under-full-employment equilibrium (how and how effectively do the various types of monetary policy affect real output or employment?) and that the economy has reached full employment with an unaccept-able rate of price inflation (how and how effectively do the various tools of monetary policy combat inflation?).

4. Solution with an Active Government

In this chapter two major questions will be examined. First, how do the major tools of monetary policy work? That is, how do these tools affect the important variables of the model (in particular, the money stock and the various rates of interest)? Second, given the effects of these monetary tools, how do they affect problems of unemployment and inflation? What are the qualitative and quantitative differences among the monetary tools?

Changes in Reserve Requirements

The reserve requirement, r, enters the model in two places. The level of required reserves and the quantity of bank loans supplied are both affected by changes in r. We have

$$R = r(D + T) \tag{4.1}$$

$$L_b^S = f_1(r)(D + T) + A_{12}\bar{r}_b \tag{4.2}$$

where we have used the function notation $f_1(r)$ to replace the term π in Equation 2.92, since this notation clearly shows the dependence of L_b^S on r. R is, of course, simply the level of required reserves. Expressions 4.1 and 4.2 indicate the effects of changes in r. Consider an increase in r, $dr > 0$. From 4.1 this has the obvious effect of increasing required reserves:

$$dR = dr(D + T). \tag{4.3}$$

The immediate impact of this increase in R is a reduction in the banks' holdings of currency, government securities, and firms' securities in an amount equal to dR:

$$dR = dr(D + T) = d(G_b + F_b + D_b). \tag{4.4}$$

We assume that the banks reduce the levels of these assets in proportion to the coefficients of $D + T$ in the banks' demand for them. That is,

$$dG_b = \frac{\rho}{\rho + \gamma + \mu} dR \tag{4.5}$$

$$dF_b = \frac{\mu}{\rho + \gamma + \mu} dR \tag{4.6}$$

$$dC_b = \frac{\gamma}{\rho + \mu + \gamma} dR. \tag{4.7}$$

Consider the banks' attempt to reduce their holdings of government securities. These securities may be purchased by either the public, the firms, the intermediaries, or the government (if it wishes to take some action to help offset the "crunch" of a change in the reserve requirement). We can then write

$$dG_b = dG_p + dG_f + dG_n + dG_g. \tag{4.8}$$

We assume that dG_g is determined by the government strictly on the basis of economic policy and may range from zero to dG_b. The amount of dG_b not absorbed by the government is divided among the private sectors in this manner:

$$dG_b - dG_g = dG_p + dG_f + dG_n$$

$$dG_p = \frac{g}{g + g_f + g_n} (dG_b - dG_g) \tag{4.9}$$

$$dG_f = \frac{g_f}{g + g_f + g_n} (dG_b - dG_g) \tag{4.10}$$

$$dG_n = \frac{g_n}{g + g_f + g_n} (dG_b - dG_g), \tag{4.11}$$

where the g's are the major parameters in the sectors' demands for government securities.

These three sectors pay for their purchases of government securities by reducing the level of all other (financial) assets they hold (except for firms' securities). The reductions in other assets for each sector are given by

$$dG_p \quad = \quad dD_{pg} + dC_{pg} + dN_{pg} + dT_{pg} \tag{4.12}$$

where

$$dD_{pg} \quad = \quad \frac{k_1}{k_1 + k_2 + k_3 + n_p} \, dG_p \tag{4.13}$$

$$dC_{pg} \quad = \quad \frac{k_2}{k_1 + k_2 + k_3 + n_p} \, dG_p \tag{4.14}$$

$$dN_{pg} \quad = \quad \frac{n_p}{k_1 + k_2 + k_3 + n_p} \, dG_p \tag{4.15}$$

$$dT_{pg} \quad = \quad \frac{k_3}{k_1 + k_2 + k_3 + n_p} \, dG_p; \tag{4.16}$$

$$dG_f \quad = \quad dD_{fg} + dC_{fg} + dN_{fg} + dT_{fg} \tag{4.17}$$

where

$$dD_{fg} \quad = \quad \frac{d_f}{d_f + a_5 + n_f + t_f} \, dG_f \tag{4.18}$$

$$dC_{fg} \quad = \quad \frac{a_5}{d_f + a_5 + n_f + t_f} \, dG_f \tag{4.19}$$

$$dN_{fg} \quad = \quad \frac{n_f}{d_f + a_5 + n_f + t_f} \, dG_f \tag{4.20}$$

$$dT_{fg} \quad = \quad \frac{t_f}{d_f + a_5 + n_f + t_f} \, dG_f; \tag{4.21}$$

and

$$dG_n \quad = \quad dD_{ng} + dC_{ng} \tag{4.22}$$

where

$$dD_{ng} = \frac{d_n}{d_n + c_n} dG_n \qquad (4.23)$$

$$dC_{ng} = \frac{c_n}{d_n + c_n} dG_n. \qquad (4.24)$$

Again, the parameters in the preceding equations are from the sectors' demands for the various assets. Ignoring for a moment the impact on interest rates, the results of this initial sale of G by the banks can be written as

$$dD_{g1} = dD_{pg} + dD_{fg} + dD_{ng}$$

$$= \frac{k_1}{k_1 + k_2 + k_3 + n_p} (dG_p) + \frac{d_f}{d_f + a_5 + n_f + t_f} (dG_f)$$

$$+ \frac{d_n}{d_n + c_n} (dG_n), \qquad (4.25)$$

where dD_{g1} means the first change in demand deposits resulting from the banks' sale of government securities. By combining 4.25 and the system 4.9 through 4.11, we can write

$$dD_{g1} = [(\frac{k_1}{k_1 + k_2 + k_3 + n_p})(\frac{g}{g + g_f + g_n}) +$$

$$(\frac{d_f}{d_f + a_5 + n_f + t_f})(\frac{g_f}{g + g_f + g_n}) +$$

$$(\frac{d_n}{d_n + c_n})(\frac{g_n}{g + g_f + g_n})] (dG_b - dG_g)$$

or

$$dD_{g1} = (\frac{k_1 g}{k_1 + k_2 + k_3 + n_p} + \frac{d_f g_f}{d_f + a_5 + n_f + t_f} + \frac{d_n g_n}{d_n + c_n})$$

$$(\frac{dG_b - dG_g}{g + g_f + g_n}). \qquad (4.26)$$

Proceeding in a similar manner we can write the expression for the initial impact on time deposits resulting from the banks' sale of government securities as

$$dT_{g1} = (\frac{k_3 g}{k_1 + k_2 + k_3 + n_p} + \frac{t_f g_f}{d_f + a_5 + n_f + t_f})$$

$$(\frac{dG_b - dG_g}{g + g_f + g_n}). \tag{4.27}$$

The expression for the initial impact on deposits in intermediaries is

$$dN_{g1} = (\frac{n_p g}{k_1 + k_2 + k_3 + n_p} + \frac{n_f g_f}{d_f + a_5 + n_f + t_f})$$

$$(\frac{dG_b - dG_g}{g + g_f + g_n}). \tag{4.28}$$

The initial impact on currency balances is given by

$$dC_{g1} = (\frac{k_2 g}{k_1 + k_2 + k_3 + n_p} + \frac{a_5 g_f}{d_f + a_5 + n_f + t_f} +$$

$$\frac{c_n g_n}{d_n + c_n})(\frac{dG_b - dG_g}{g + g_f + g_n}). \tag{4.29}$$

We now examine the initial impact of the banks' sale of firms' securities:

$$dF_b = \frac{\mu}{\rho + \mu + \gamma} \, dR = dF_p + dF_n. \tag{4.30}$$

Proceeding in an analogous manner,

$$dF_p = \frac{f}{f + b_n} \, dF_b \tag{4.31}$$

$$dF_n = \frac{b_n}{f + b_n} \, dF_b. \tag{4.32}$$

These purchases of firms' securities by the public and the intermediaries causes a further reduction in their other assets, given by

$$dF_p = dD_{pf} + dC_{pf} + dN_{pf} + dT_{pf} \tag{4.33}$$

where

$$dD_{pf} = \frac{k_1}{k_1 + k_2 + k_3 + n_p} \, dF_p \tag{4.34}$$

$$dC_{pf} = \frac{k_2}{k_1 + k_2 + k_3 + n_p} \, dF_p \tag{4.35}$$

$$dN_{pf} = \frac{n_p}{k_1 + k_2 + k_3 + n_p} \, dF_p \tag{4.36}$$

$$dT_{pf} = \frac{k_3}{k_1 + k_2 + k_3 + n_p} \, dF_p \, ; \tag{4.37}$$

$$dF_{nf} = dD_{nf} + dC_{nf} \tag{4.38}$$

where

$$dD_{nf} = \frac{d_n}{d_n + c_n} \, dF_n \tag{4.39}$$

$$dC_{nf} = \frac{c_n}{d_n + c_n} \, dF_n . \tag{4.40}$$

The initial impacts resulting from the banks' sale of firms' securities are given by

$$dD_{f1} = \left(\frac{k_1 f}{k_1 + k_2 + k_3 + n_p} + \frac{d_n b_n}{d_n + c_n}\right) \frac{dF_b}{f + b_n} \tag{4.41}$$

$$dT_{f1} = \left(\frac{k_3 f}{k_1 + k_2 + k_3 + n_p}\right) \frac{dF_b}{f + b_n} \tag{4.42}$$

$$dC_{f1} = \left(\frac{k_2 f}{k_1 + k_2 + k_3 + n_p} + \frac{c_n b_n}{d_n + c_n}\right) \frac{F_b}{f + b_n} \tag{4.43}$$

$$dN_{f1} = \left(\frac{n_p f}{k_1 + k_2 + k_3 + n_p}\right) \frac{F_b}{f + b_n} . \tag{4.44}$$

The total initial impacts on D, T, C, and N are obtained by simply adding the appropriate pairs of equations and simplifying.

$$dD_1 = 4.41 + 4.26$$

$$= \left[\frac{k_1}{k_1 + k_2 + k_3 + n_p} \, (g + f) + \frac{d_n}{c_n + d_n} \, (g_n + b_n)\right]$$

$$\left[\frac{dG_b - dG_g}{g + g_f + g_n} + \frac{dF_b}{f + b_n}\right] + \left(\frac{d_f g_f}{d_f + a_5 + n_f + t_f}\right)$$

$$\left(\frac{dG_b - dG_g}{g + g_f + g_n}\right). \tag{4.45}$$

$$dT_1 \quad = \quad 4.42 + 4.27$$

$$= \left(\frac{k_3 (f + g)}{k_1 + k_2 + k_3 + g_n}\right)\left(\frac{dG_b - dG_g}{g + g_f + g_n} + \frac{dF_b}{f + b_n}\right)$$

$$\left(\frac{t_f g_f}{d_f + a_5 + n_f + t_f}\right)\left(\frac{dG_b - dG_g}{g + g_f + g_n}\right). \tag{4.46}$$

$$dC_1 = 4.29 + 4.43$$

$$= \left(\frac{k_2 (f + g)}{k_1 + k_2 + k_3 + n_p} + \frac{c_n (b_n + g_n)}{c_n + d_n}\right)$$

$$\left(\frac{F_b}{f + b_n} + \frac{dG_b - dG_g}{g + g_f + g_n}\right) + \left(\frac{a_5 g_r}{d_f + a_5 + n_f + t_f}\right)$$

$$\left(\frac{dG_b - dG_g}{g + g_f + g_n}\right). \tag{4.47}$$

$$dN_1 = 4.28 + 4.44$$

$$= \left(\frac{n_p (f + g)}{k_1 + k_2 + k_3 + n_p}\right)\left(\frac{F_b}{f + b_n} + \frac{dG_b - dG_g}{g + g_f + g_n}\right)$$

$$+ \left(\frac{n_f g_f}{d_f + a_5 + n_f + t_f}\right)\left(\frac{dG_b - dG_g}{g + g_f + g_n}\right). \tag{4.48}$$

The sum of 4.45 and 4.46 gives the initial reduction in bank deposits. This, of course, results in another reserve deficiency for the banks and thus initiates another round of asset adjustment throughout the economy. The new level of required reserves is given by

$$R \text{ new} = (r + dr) [D + T - (dD + dT)],$$

while actual reserves are now

$$R \text{ actual} = (r + dr)(D + T) - (dD + dT),$$

so that the reserve deficiency is the difference between these two expressions, or

$$R \text{ def} = (dD + dT)[1 - (r + dr)]. \tag{4.49}$$

In terms of Equations 4.45 and 4.46

$$R \text{ def} = \left\{ \left[\frac{(k_1 + k_3)(g + f)}{k_1 + k_2 + k_3 + n_p} + \frac{d_n}{c_n + d_n}(g_n + b_n) \right] \right.$$

$$\left[\frac{dG_b - dG_g}{g + g_f + g_n} + \frac{dF_b}{f + b_n} \right] +$$

$$\left. \left[\left(\frac{g_f(d_f + t_f)}{d_f + a_s + n_f + t_f} \right) \left(\frac{dG_b - dG_g}{g + g_f + g_n} \right) \right] \right\}$$

$$\left\{ 1 - (r + dr) \right\} . \tag{4.50}$$

Note that Equation 4.50 can be written as

$$R \text{ def} = \left[\left(\frac{k_1 + k_3}{k_1 + k_2 + k_3 + n_p} \right)(dG_p + dF_p) + \right.$$

$$\frac{d_f + t_f}{d_f + a_s + n_f + t_f} dG_f + \left(\frac{d_n}{c_n + d_n} \right)$$

$$(dG_n + dF_n) \Big] [1 - (r + dr)], \tag{4.51}$$

where each term on the right-hand side is the size of one of the nonbank private sector's reduction of its holding of demand and time deposits. Furthermore, we know that

$$dG_p = \left(\frac{g}{g + g_f + g_n} \right) \left[\left(\frac{\rho}{\rho + \mu + \gamma} \right)(dr(D + T)) - dG_g \right] \tag{4.52}$$

$$dG_f = \left(\frac{g_f}{g + g_f + g_n} \right) \left[\left(\frac{\rho}{\rho + \gamma + \mu} \right)(dr(D + T)) - dG_g \right] \tag{4.53}$$

$$dG_n = (\frac{g_n}{g + g_f + g_n}) \ [(\frac{\rho}{\rho + \gamma + \mu}) \ (dr(D + T)) - dG_g] \qquad (4.54)$$

$$dF_p = (\frac{f}{f + b_n}) \ (\frac{\mu}{\rho + \gamma + \mu}) \ dr(D + T) \qquad (4.55)$$

$$dF_n = (\frac{b_n}{f + b_n}) \ (\frac{\mu}{\rho + \gamma + \mu}) \ dr(D + T). \qquad (4.56)$$

R def results in another reduction of the banks' holdings of government securities, firms' securities, and currency which, in turn, causes another rearrangement of the asset portfolios of the various sectors. This complex process continues, forming an infinite series of changes in assets. The solution revolves around these two problems: finding the general expression for the series of reserve deficiencies, and finding whether or not this series converges and, if so, to what.

We introduce the following notation:

$$R \ def \ 1 = dr(D + T)$$

$$R \ def \ 2 = [(\frac{k_1 + k_3}{k_1 + k_2 + k_3 + n_p}) \ (dG_p + dF_p) +$$

$$\frac{d_f + t_f}{d_f + a_5 + n_f + t_f} \ dG_f + (\frac{d_n}{c_n + d_n})$$

$$(dG_n + dF_n)] \ [1 - (r + dr)].$$

By substituting 4.52 through 4.56 into 4.51, we obtain

$$\frac{R \ def \ 2}{1 - (r + dr)} = (\frac{k_1 + k_3}{k_1 + k_2 + k_3 + n_p}) \ \{(\frac{g}{g + g_f + g_n})$$

$$[(\frac{\rho}{\rho + \gamma + \mu}) \ R \ def \ 1 - dG_g] + (\frac{f}{f + b_n})$$

$$(\frac{\mu}{\rho + \gamma + \mu}) \ R \ def \} + (\frac{d_f + t_f}{a_5 + d_f + n_f + t_f})$$

$$\Biggl\{ (\frac{g_f}{g + g_f + g_n}) \; [(\frac{\rho}{\rho + \gamma + \mu}) \; (R \; def \; 1)$$

$$- \; dG_g] \Biggr\} \; + (\frac{d_n}{c_n + d_n}) \; \Biggl\} \; (\frac{g_n}{g + g_f + g_n})$$

$$[(\frac{\rho}{\rho + \mu + \gamma}) \; (R \; def) \; - \; dG_g] \; + (\frac{b_n}{f + b_n})$$

$$(\frac{\mu}{\rho + \gamma + \mu}) \; R \; def \Biggr\} \qquad (4.57)$$

In order to simplify the analysis, we assume that after its first purchase of government securities, the government purchases no more from the banking system while the readjustment process is working itself out. This assumption permits us to write the general expression for any reserve deficiency as

$$R \; def \; j = [(\frac{k_1 + k_3}{k_1 + k_2 + k_3 + n_p}) \; (dG_{pj} + dF_{pj}) \; +$$

$$\frac{d_f + t_f}{d_f + a_s + n_f + t_f} \; (dG_{fj}) \; + \frac{d_n}{c_n + d_n}$$

$$(dG_{nf} + dF_{nj})] \; [1 - (r + dr)], \qquad (4.58)$$

where, because of our assumptions about the government,

$$dG_{pj} = (\frac{g}{g + g_f + g_n}) \; (\frac{\rho}{\rho + \gamma + \mu}) \; R \; def \; j \; - \; 1$$

$$dG_{fj} = (\frac{g_f}{g + g_f + g_n}) \; (\frac{\rho}{\rho + \gamma + \mu}) \; R \; def \; j \; - \; 1$$

$$dG_{nj} = (\frac{g_n}{g + g_f + g_n}) \; (\frac{\rho}{\rho + \gamma + \mu}) \; R \; def \; j \; - \; 1$$

$$dF_{pj} = (\frac{f}{f + b_n}) \; (\frac{\mu}{\rho + \gamma + \mu}) \; R \; def \; j \; - \; 1$$

$$dF_{nj} = \left(\frac{b_n}{f + b_n}\right)\left(\frac{\mu}{\rho + \gamma + \mu}\right) R \text{ def } j - 1.$$

Substituting these expressions into 4.58 and dividing through by R def j
− 1, we have

$$\frac{R \text{ def } j}{R \text{ def } j - 1} = \frac{k_1 + k_2}{k_1 + k_2 + k_3 + n_p} \left[\left(\frac{g}{g + g_f + g_n}\right)\right.$$

$$\left(\frac{\rho}{\rho + \gamma + \mu}\right) + \left(\frac{f}{f + b_n}\right)\left(\frac{\mu}{\rho + \gamma + \mu}\right)\Big] +$$

$$\left(\frac{d_f + t_f}{d_f + a_s + n_f + t_f}\right)\left(\frac{g_f}{g + g_f + g_n}\right)$$

$$\left(\frac{\rho}{\rho + \gamma + \mu}\right) + \frac{d_n}{c_n + d_n}\left[\left(\frac{g_n}{g + g_f + g_n}\right)\right.$$

$$\left(\frac{\rho}{\rho + \gamma + \mu}\right) + \left(\frac{b_n}{f + b_n}\right)\left(\frac{\mu}{\rho + \gamma + \mu}\right)\Big]$$

$$[1 - (r + dr)]. \tag{4.59}$$

This result holds for all R def j, j > 4. Call this ratio of reserve
deficiences Q_r. Then it follows that

$$\frac{R \text{ def } 4}{R \text{ def } 3} = Q_r \Rightarrow R \text{ def } 4 = Q_r R \text{ def } 3$$

$$\frac{R \text{ def } 5}{R \text{ def } 4} = Q_r \Rightarrow R \text{ def } 5 = Q_r^2 R \text{ def } 3$$

.

.

.

$$\frac{R \text{ def } i}{R \text{ def } i - 1} = Q_r \Rightarrow R \text{ def } i = Q_r^{i-3} R \text{ def } 3.$$

The expression for the total reserve deficiency, R def T, can be written as

$$\text{R def T} = \text{R def 1} + \text{R def 2} + \text{R def 3} + \sum_{i=4}^{\infty} \text{R def i}$$

(4.60)

$$= \text{R def 1} + \text{R def 2} + \text{R def 3} + \lim_{n \to \infty} \sum_{j=1}^{n} Q_r^j \text{R def 3}.$$

This infinite series will converge to R def $3/1 - Q_r$ if $|Q_r| < 1$. Since each term individually in Q_r is less than 1, Q_r will be less than 1 due to its multiplicative structure. (If Q_r were greater than 1, any change in the reserve requirement would have an infinitely large impact on the economy since the total excess or deficit in reserves would be infinitely large [small].)

We can write the total reserve deficiency as

$$\text{R def T} = \text{R def 1} + \text{R def 2} + \text{R def 3} \left(1 + \frac{1}{1 - Q_r}\right)$$

(4.61)

where

$$\text{R def 3} = Q \left\{ \left(\frac{k_1 + k_3}{k_1 + k_2 + k_3 + n_p}\right) \left[\left(\frac{g}{g + g_f + g_n}\right) \right.\right.$$

$$\left(\frac{\rho}{\rho + \gamma + \mu}\right) \text{dr(D + T)} + \left(\frac{f}{f + b_n}\right) \left(\frac{\mu}{\rho + \gamma + \mu}\right) \text{dr(D + T)}]$$

$$+ \left(\frac{d_f + t_f}{a_s + d_f + n_f + t_f}\right) \left[\left(\frac{g_f}{g + g_f + g_n}\right)\right.$$

$$\left(\frac{\rho}{\rho + \gamma + \mu}\right) \text{dr(D + T)} + \left(\frac{d_n}{c_n + d_n}\right)][\left(\frac{\rho}{\rho + \gamma + \mu}\right)$$

$$\left(\frac{g_n}{g + g_f + g_n}\right) + \left(\frac{b_n}{b_n + c_n}\right) \left(\frac{\mu}{\rho + \gamma + \mu}\right)] \right\}$$

$$[1 - (r + \text{dr})].$$

(4.62)

There seems little reason to write 4.61 out in full except to underscore the complexity added when a model of the money mechanism is made just a bit more realistic.

From the expression for R def T we can derive all of the remaining impacts on assets from the change in reserve requirements. The banks' decreases in assets are given by

$$dC_{bt} = \frac{\gamma}{\rho + \gamma + \mu} \text{ R def T} \tag{4.63}$$

$$dG_{bt} = \frac{\rho}{\rho + \gamma + \mu} \text{ R def T} \tag{4.64}$$

$$dF_{bt} = \frac{\mu}{\rho + \gamma + \mu} \text{ R def T.} \tag{4.65}$$

The corresponding increases in government and firms' securities held by the other sectors are given by:

$$dG_{pt} = \frac{g}{g + g_f + g_n} \left(\frac{\rho}{\rho + \gamma + \mu} \text{ R def T} - dG_{go} \right) \tag{4.66}$$

$$dG_{nt} = \frac{g_n}{g + g_f + g_n} \left(\frac{\rho}{\rho + \gamma + \mu} \text{ R def T} - dG_{go} \right) \tag{4.67}$$

$$dG_{ft} = \frac{g_f}{g + g_f + g_n} \left(\frac{\rho}{\rho + \gamma + \mu} \text{ R def T} - dG_{go} \right) \tag{4.68}$$

$$dF_{pt} = \frac{f}{f + b_n} \left(\frac{\mu}{\rho + \gamma + \mu} \text{ R def T} \right) \tag{4.69}$$

$$dF_{nt} = \frac{b_n}{f + b_n} \left(\frac{\mu}{\rho + \gamma + \mu} \text{ R def T} \right). \tag{4.70}$$

The public's increase in assets is the sum of 4.66 and 4.69, or

$$d(G + F)_{pt} = \frac{g}{g + g_n + g_f} \left(\frac{\rho}{\rho + \gamma + \mu} \text{ R def T} - dG_{go} \right) +$$

$$\frac{f}{f + b_n} \left(\frac{\mu}{\rho + \gamma + \mu} \text{ R def T} \right). \tag{4.71}$$

The intermediaries' holdings of government and firms' securities increase by

$$d(G + F)_{nt} = \frac{g_n}{g + g_f + g_n} \left(\frac{\rho}{\rho + \gamma + \mu} R \text{ def } T - dG_{go} \right) +$$

$$\frac{b_n}{f + b_n} \left(\frac{\mu}{\rho + \gamma + \mu} R \text{ def } T \right). \tag{4.72}$$

The firms' increases in assets are simply Equation 4.68.
The offsetting decreases in assets for the public sector are

$$dC_{pt} = \frac{k_2}{k_1 + k_2 + k_3 + n_p} d(G + F)_{pt} \tag{4.73}$$

$$dD_{pt} = \frac{k_1}{k_1 + k_2 + k_3 + n_p} d(G + F)_{pt} \tag{4.74}$$

$$dT_{pt} = \frac{k_3}{k_1 + k_2 + k_3 + n_p} d(G + F)_{pt} \tag{4.75}$$

$$dN_{pt} = \frac{n_p}{k_1 + k_2 + k_3 + n_p} d(G + F)_{pt}. \tag{4.76}$$

The intermediaries' reductions in assets are

$$dC_{nt} = \frac{c_n}{c_n + d_n} d(G + F)_{nt} \tag{4.77}$$

$$dD_{nt} = \frac{d_n}{c_n + d_n} d(G + F)_{nt}. \tag{4.78}$$

The firms' reductions in assets are

$$dC_{ft} = \frac{a_5}{d_f + a_5 + n_f + t_f} dG_{ft} \tag{4.79}$$

$$dD_{ft} = \frac{d_f}{d_f + a_5 + n_f + t_f} dG_{ft} \tag{4.80}$$

$$dT_{ft} = \frac{t_f}{d_f + a_5 + n_f + t_f} dG_{ft} \tag{4.81}$$

$$dN_{ft} = \frac{n_f}{d_f + a_5 + n_f + t_f} \, dG_{ft}. \tag{4.82}$$

We can at last find expressions for the total reductions in assets, caused by the change in reserve requirements:

$$dC_t = 4.63 + 4.73 + 4.77 + 4.80$$

$$= \frac{\gamma}{\rho + \gamma + \mu} \, R \, \text{def} \, T + \frac{k_2}{k_1 + k_2 + k_3 + n_p} \, d(G + F)_{pt} +$$

$$\frac{c_n}{c_n + d_n} \, d(G + F)_{nt} + \frac{a_5}{d_f + a_5 + n_f + t_f} \, dG_{ft} \tag{4.83}$$

$$dD_t = 4.74 + 4.78 + 4.80$$

$$= \frac{k_1}{k_1 + k_2 + k_3 + n_p} \, d(G + F)_{pt} + \frac{d_n}{c_n + d_n} \, d(G + F)_{nt} +$$

$$\frac{d_f}{d_f + a_5 + n_f + t_f} dG_{ft} \tag{4.84}$$

$$dT_t = 4.75 + 4.81$$

$$= \frac{k_3}{k_1 + k_2 + k_3 + n_p} \, d(G + F)_{pt} + \frac{t_f}{d_f + a_5 + n_f + t_f} \, dG_{ft}$$

$$\tag{4.85}$$

$$dN_t = 4.76 + 4.82$$

$$= \frac{n_p}{k_1 + k_2 + k_3 + n_p} \, d(G + F)_{pt} + \frac{n_f}{d_f + a_5 + n_f + t_f} \, dG_{ft}.$$

$$\tag{4.86}$$

The total impact on the money stock of the increase in reserve requirements is simply the sum of 4.83 and 4.84:

$$dM_{tr} = d(C_t + D_t) = \frac{\gamma}{\rho + \gamma + \mu} \, R \, \text{def} \, T +$$

$$[\frac{k_2 + k_1}{k_1 + k_2 + k_3 + n_p}] \, d(G + F)_{pt} + d(G + F)_{nt}$$

$$+ [\frac{a_5 + d_f}{d_f + a_5 + n_f + t_f}] \, dG_{ft}, \tag{4.87}$$

which is, of course, negative in the case of increases in the reserve requirement. This same expression holds for the case of reductions in r, in which case it will be positive.

Nothing has been said yet about the changes in the prices of government and firms' securities necessary to induce the various nonbank sectors either to buy or sell the amounts necessary for the relations just developed to hold. Without the appropriate changes in prices (rates of interest), the asset readjustment process just described cannot occur. Again, we will consider the case of an increase in reserve requirements. (In the opposite case, the argument is essentially the same with only the signs changed.) The question here is by how much must the prices of government and firms' securities fall (the rates increase) to induce the various nonbank sectors to increase their holdings of G and F as given by Equations 4.68, 4.72, and 4.73? (Note that the effects of a change in the reserve requirement on the rates on time deposits and deposits in the intermediaries will not be direct, but will be a result of the effect of dr on r_g and r_f. As these rates increase, r_t and r_n will tend to follow.) The aggregate demand for G and F (excluding the banks' demand) can be written as

$$G_a^D = gY + A_{26}\bar{r}_p + g_nN + A_{15}\bar{r}_n + g_f(PX) + A_7\bar{r}_f \tag{4.88}$$

$$F_a^D = b_nN + A_{17}\bar{r}_n + n_pY + A_{30}\bar{r}_p. \tag{4.89}$$

Writing these expressions in terms of only the variables that are directly affected as a result of the change in the reserve requirement, we have

$$G_a^D = (a_7 + a_{15} + a_{26})r_f + (b_7 + b_{15} + b_{26})r_g + g_nN \tag{4.90}$$

$$F_a^D = (a_{17} + a_{30})r_f + (b_{17} + b_{30})r_g + b_nN. \tag{4.91}$$

The immediate changes in r_f, r_g, and N must be such that $dG_a^D = 4.66 + 4.67 + 4.68 = (\mu/\rho + \gamma + \mu) \, R \, def \, T$. We already know that the total change in N is given by

$$dN_t = \frac{n_p}{k_1 + k_2 + k_3 + n_p} \, d(G + F)_{pt} + \frac{n_f}{d_f + a_5 + n_f + t_f} \, dG_{ft}.$$

(4.86)

Thus,

$$dG_a^D = \frac{\rho}{\rho + \gamma + \mu} \, R \text{ def } T = (a_7 + a_{15} + a_{26})dr_f +$$

$$(b_7 + b_{15} + b_{26})dr_g$$

(4.92)

$$dF_a^D = \frac{\mu}{\rho + \gamma + \mu} \, R \text{ def } T = (a_{17} + a_{30})dr_f + (b_{17} +$$

$$b_{30})dr_g + b_n dN.$$

(4.93)

Substituting the expression for dN into 4.82 and 4.83 yields a system of two equations in two unknowns, dr_g and dr_f. Solving this system simultaneously yields expressions for the necessary increases in dr_g and dr_f:

$$dr_{gr} = R \text{ def } T \, [\frac{\rho}{\rho + \gamma + \mu} - \frac{a_7 + a_{15} + a_{26}}{a_{17} + a_{30}}$$

$$\frac{(\frac{\mu}{\rho + \gamma + \mu})] + dN(g_n + b_n)(\frac{a_7 + a_{15} + a_{26}}{a_{17} + a_{30}})}{b_7 + b_{15} + b_{26} - \frac{a_7 + a_{15} + a_{26}}{a_{17} + a_{30}} (b_{17} + b_{30})}$$

(4.94)

$$dr_{fr} = \frac{R \text{ def } T}{a_{17} + a_{30}} \left\{ \frac{\mu}{\rho + \gamma + \mu} - (b_{17} + b_{30}) \right.$$

$$\left[\frac{\frac{\rho}{\rho + \gamma + \mu} - (\frac{a_7 + a_{15} + a_{26}}{a_{17} + a_{30}}) \frac{\mu}{\rho + \gamma + \mu}}{b_7 + b_{15} + b_{26} - (b_{17} + b_{30})} \right] \right\}$$

$$\frac{dN}{a_{17} + a_{30}} \left\{ b_n - (b_{17} + b_{30}) \right.$$

$$\left[\frac{\dfrac{b_n(a_7 + a_{15} + a_{26})}{a_{17} + a_{30}} - g_n}{b_7 + b_{15} + b_{26} - (b_{17} + b_{30})} \right] \Biggr\} \tag{4.95}$$

The expressions for dM_{tr}, dr_{gr}, and dr_{fr} provide the necessary information to calculate the other effects on the economy of the asset readjustment resulting from a change in the reserve requirement, r. To calculate the effects on income, for example, one need only combine the expressions developed in the last chapter for $\partial Y/\partial M$, $\partial Y/\partial r_g$, and $\partial Y/\partial r_f$ with the value of the appropriate differential to obtain the three effects on income caused by the change in r: the money-induced effect, $\partial Y/\partial M \ dM_{tr}$; the government security rate-induced effect, $\partial Y/\partial r_g \ dr_{gr}$; and the firms' securities rate-induced effect, $\partial Y/\partial r_f \ dr_{fr}$. The same procedure can be followed to obtain expressions for the effect on prices, outputs, and the other rates of interest.

Changes in the reserve requirement also affect the economy in another manner. The foregoing concentrated solely on changes resulting from a readjustment in the asset portfolios of the various sectors. Other effects work through the impact of a change in r on the banks' willingness to supply loans to both the public and the firms. Equation 4.2 ($L_b^S = f_1(r)(D + T) + A_{12}\bar{r}_b$) serves as the basis for discussing these effects. Taking the total differential of 4.2, we obtain

$$dL_b^S = f_1(r) \ \frac{\partial(D + T)}{\partial r} \ dr + (D + T) \ \frac{\partial f_1}{\partial r} \ dr$$

$$+ A_{12} \ \frac{\partial \bar{r}_b}{\partial r} \ dr. \tag{4.96}$$

The quantity supplied of bank loans is reduced by an increase in r, ceteris paribus, for three reasons: an increase in r reduces $D + T$ ($\partial(D + T)/\partial r < 0$) (this impact on $D + T$ has been discussed); an increase in r reduces the amount that may be lent per dollar of deposits ($\partial f_1/\partial r < 0$); and an increase in r increases the rates on securities held as secondary reserves which, without an increase in loan rates, reduces the amount banks are willing to lend per dollar of deposits (a_{12} and $b_{12} < 0$ combined with $\partial r_f/\partial r$ and $\partial r_g/\partial r > 0$).

Likewise, the quantity of loans demanded by the public and the firms will be reduced when r is increased, since interest rates will move higher while income, prices, and real output tend to fall as the money stock shrinks. Consequently, the actual amount of loans will fall, which will, in turn, lower the demand for both the consumer and capital good, thus further depressing the economy's level of economic activity.

These effects on loans and demands could be calculated exactly in terms of the model, but the chain of causality seems so clear that this will not be done. It is sufficient to say that the expressions developed earlier, when only the asset readjustment effects of a change in r were considered, understate the various impacts of a change in r on the economy since they do not take into account the impact of dr on either the quantity of loans demanded or the quantity supplied.

In quick summary, it has been shown that changes in the reserve requirement affect the economy through two major channels: by causing a readjustment in the asset portfolios of the various sectors of the economy, and by influencing the amount of loans made and thus the demand for goods. Working through both these avenues, changes in the reserve requirement are a powerful and diffuse technique for influencing the level of activity in our economy.

CHANGES IN THE REDISCOUNT RATE

The banks' demand for rediscounting is given by

$$d^d = \overline{L}_p^{Db} + \overline{L}_f^{Db} - \overline{L}_b^{S} - \frac{d_o}{r_{bp} - r_d} - \frac{d_1}{r_{bf} - r_{dt}} \qquad (2.101)$$

where

$$d^d > 0 \text{ when } \overline{L}_p^{Db} + \overline{L}_f^{Db} > \overline{L}_b^{S} + \frac{d_o}{r_{bp} - r_d} + \frac{d_1}{r_{bf} - r_d}$$

and $d^d = 0$ otherwise.

No matter how great the difference between the rates on loans and the rediscount rate, no rediscounting occurs unless there is an excess demand for loans.

There are two cases to consider when examining the effects of changes in the rediscount rate. First, there may be an excess supply of loans. In this case, neither increases nor reductions in r_d will have any effect on the economy, since the change in r_d will not cause a change in the actual amount of loans, nor will banks have, solely because of the change in r_d, any reason to change the rates on loans (even though these will tend to fall not as a result of a change in r_d, but because of the excess supply of loans). Second, there may be either an excess demand for loans or a situation of equilibrium in the bank loan market. I want to show that in this case changes in r_d will have an impact on the economy. Note that the terms excess demand and excess supply of loans are used to refer to the difference between the aggregate quantity of loans demanded, $L_p^{Db} + L_f^{Db}$, and the quantity of loans supplied out of unborrowed reserves, $\bar{L}_b^S$. When $L_p^{Db} + L_f^{Db} > \bar{L}_b^S$, the possibility exists that the bank will engage in some rediscounting; the actual amount will not, in general, be equal to this difference.

Examination of 2.101 shows that, since d_0 and d_1 are positive constants, increases in r_d lower the amount of rediscounting banks are willing to engage in while reductions in r_d increase d^d, ceteris paribus. Differentiating 2.101 with respect to r_d yields

$$\frac{\partial d^d}{\partial r_d} = \frac{\partial L_p^{Db}}{\partial r_d} + \frac{\partial L_f^{Db}}{\partial r} - \frac{\partial L_b^S}{\partial r} + \frac{d_0 \left(\dfrac{\partial r_{bp}}{\partial r_d} - 1 \right)}{(r_{bp} - r_d)^2} +$$

$$\frac{d_1 \left(\dfrac{\partial r_{bf}}{\partial r_d} - 1 \right)}{(r_{bp} - r_d)^2} . \tag{4.97}$$

$\partial d^d / \partial r_d$ is negative.

1. $\partial L_p^{Db} / \partial r_d$ and $\partial L_f^{Db} / \partial r_d$ are negative because increases in r_d tend to increase r_{bp} and r_{bf}, thus lowering the quantity of loans demanded;

2. $\partial \bar{L}_b^S / \partial r_d$ is positive since increases in r_{bp} and r_{bf} will increase the quantity of loans supplied;

3. both $\partial r_{bp} / \partial r_d$ and $\partial r_{bf} / \partial r_d$ are positive but less than or equal to 1.[1]

The effects of both increases and decreases in r_d under the possibilities of (1) prior equilibrium in the loan market and (2) prior excess demand in the loan market will now be considered.

1. If $\partial r_{bp} / \partial r_b$ and $\partial r_{bf} / \partial r_d$ were greater than 1 (this is, of course, an empirical question), we have the "perverse" case where an increase in r_d has such a strong impact on the rates banks charge that this induces them to increase their amount of rediscounting. (Remember we are discussing a situation where there may be an excess demand for loans. In such a situation, the "perverse" result is perhaps less unlikely.)

By equilibrium in the bank loan market it is meant that the actual amount lent to each sector is equal to its quantity of loans demanded from the bank. This equality may or may not have been achieved through rediscounting by the banks. Consider first an increase in r_d coupled with equilibrium in the loan market. If equilibrium were previously achieved without rediscounting, an increase in r_d will have no impact on the economy since, ceteris paribus, the actual amounts lent and rates on bank loans will be unchanged. If, however, equilibrium were reached through rediscounting, the increase in r_d will reduce the amount of rediscounting the banks are willing to engage in, thus causing a reduction in the amounts actually lent to the other sectors. This raises the rates on bank loans and increases the firms' and public's demands for loans from the intermediaries. If the intermediaries are unable to accommodate this increase in the quantity of loans demanded, total loans in the economy will fall, reducing income and the output of goods. Interest rates tend to rise. In the situation under discussion, a reduction in r_d will have no effect on the economy since the reduction in r_d will not cause either the public or the firms to increase the quantity of loans they demand.

Consider a situation of excess demand for loans. Here, when r_d is increased, the actual amount of rediscounting will fall, increasing the excess demand for loans, thereby driving r_{bp} and r_{bf} higher. These increases in turn result in increases in all other rates of interest. As a result, income and the output of goods will fall. On the other hand, a reduction in r_d in this situation will increase the amount of rediscounting and thus the amount of loans actually made. This has the effect of increasing the demand for both capital and consumer goods, raising prices and output. The reduction in r_d also reduces the upward pressure on the loan rates which, in turn, tends to dampen down the increases in all other rates of interest. The effect is a general stimulation of economic activity.

In many circumstances, changes in r_d have no effect on the economy. Even in the event that it does, the resulting changes in the level of economic activity are likely to be minor unless the change in r_d is very large. The effects are also transitory in the sense that any change resulting from a change in r_d will be swamped by the effects of other changes occurring in the economy. As shown in Table 10, changes in r_d have an impact on the economy only in disequilibrium situations (and only in particular sorts of disequilibria). In cases 6 and 8 in Table 10, rates of interest are being bid up by the excess demand for loans. Unless

r_d is reduced enough to eliminate completely this excess demand, the total result in each case will be an increase in the rates of interest and either an unchanged or decreased amount lent by the banks. Only in case 7 in the table does the change in r_d reinforce the major current of change in the economy. More will be seen of this in comparing the effectiveness of the various tools of monetary policy. These effects are summarized in Table 10.

TABLE 10. Effects of Δr_d

Situation	Δr_d	Effect
1. $L_p^{Db} + L_f^{Db} < \overline{L}_b^S$	↑	None
2. $L_p^{Db} + L_f^{Db} < \overline{L}_b^S$	↓	None
3. $L_p^{Db} + L_f^{Db} > \overline{L}_b^S$ $d^d = 0$	↑	None
4. $L_p^{Db} + L_f^{Db} > \overline{L}_b^S$ $d^d = 0$	↓	None
5. $L_p^{Db} + L_f^{Db} > \overline{L}_b^S$ $d^d = 0$	↑	None
6. $L_p^{Db} + L_f^{Db} > \overline{L}_b^S$ $d^d = 0$	↓	Actual amounts lent ↑ => income, output ↑ ; interest rates ↓[a]
7. $L_p^{Db} + L_f^{Db} > \overline{L}_b^S$ $d^d > 0$	↑	Actual amounts lent ↓ => income, output ↓ ; interest rates ↑
8. $L_p^{Db} + L_f^{Db} > \overline{L}_b^S$ $d^d > 0$	↓	Actual amounts lent ↑ => income, output ↑ ; interest rates ↓[a]

a. As long as there is an excess demand for loans, interest rates tend to increase. When r_d falls, these increases are less than they would have been without the reduction in r_d.

OPEN-MARKET OPERATIONS

To this point the government has been a passive supplier-absorber of government securities. It has not consciously attempted to influence the level of economic activity by buying or selling government securities.[2]

2. I have allowed for government purchases or sales of government securities in the first section in conjunction with changes in the reserve requirement.

In this section the economic impact of such activity by the government will be considered.

Government purchases or sales of government securities affect the economy through two routes: their impact on the rate of interest on government securities, and their impact on the level of bank reserves. Since these are also the primary routes through which changes in the reserve requirement affect the economy, this analysis will be similar to that in the first section of this chapter.

Consider first a sale by the government of G* dollars worth of government securities. For simplicity, it is assumed that this amount is purchased initially by each sector in proportion to the major parameter in its demand function for government securities. Thus,

$$G^* = dG_p + dG_f + dG_n + dG_b \tag{4.98}$$

where

$$dG_p = \frac{g}{g + g_f + g_n + \rho} G^* \tag{4.99}$$

$$dG_f = \frac{g_f}{g + g_f + g_n + \rho} G^* \tag{4.100}$$

$$dG_n = \frac{g_n}{g + g_f + g_n + \rho} G^* \tag{4.101}$$

$$dG_b = \frac{\rho}{g + g_f + g_n + \rho} G^*. \tag{4.102}$$

The increased holdings of G require each sector to reduce the level of other assets it holds. Thus,

$$dG_p = dC_p + dD_p + dF_p + dT_p + dN_p \tag{4.103}$$

$$dG_f = dC_f + dD_f + dT_f + dN_f \tag{4.104}$$

$$dG_n = dC_n + dD_n + dF_n \tag{4.105}$$

$$dG_b = dC_b + dF_b. \tag{4.106}$$

For each sector we can write:

$$dC_p = \frac{k_2}{k_1 + k_2 + k_3 + n_p + f} \, dG_p \tag{4.107}$$

$$dD_p = \frac{k_1}{k_1 + k_2 + k_3 + n_p + f} \, dG_p \tag{4.108}$$

$$dF_p = \frac{f}{k_1 + k_2 + k_3 + n_p + f} \, dG_p \tag{4.109}$$

$$dT_p = \frac{k_3}{k_1 + k_2 + k_3 + n_p + f} \, dG_p \tag{4.110}$$

$$dN_p = \frac{n_p}{k_1 + k_2 + k_3 + n_p + f} \, dG_p \tag{4.111}$$

$$dC_f = \frac{a_5}{a_5 + d_f + t_f + n_f} \, dG_f \tag{4.112}$$

$$dD_f = \frac{d_f}{a_5 + d_f + t_f + n_f} \, dG_f \tag{4.113}$$

$$dT_f = \frac{t_f}{a_5 + d_f + t_f + n_f} \, dG_f \tag{4.114}$$

$$dN_f = \frac{n_f}{a_5 + d_f + t_f + n_f} \, dG_f \tag{4.115}$$

$$dC_n = \frac{c_n}{c_n + d_n + b_n} \, dG_n \tag{4.116}$$

$$dD_n = \frac{d_n}{c_n + d_n + b_n} \, dG_n \tag{4.117}$$

$$dF_n = \frac{f_n}{c_n + d_n + b_n} \, dG_n \tag{4.118}$$

$$dC_b = \frac{\gamma}{\gamma + \mu} \, dG_b \tag{4.119}$$

$$dF_b = \frac{\mu}{\gamma + \mu} \, dG_b \, . \tag{4.120}$$

The immediate result of this first round readjustment in assets is that deposits in the banks have been reduced by

$$d(D + T) = dD_p + dD_f + dD_n + dT_p + dT_f$$

$$= \frac{k_1 + k_3}{k_1 + k_2 + k_3 + n_p + f} \, (dG_p) +$$

$$\frac{d_f + t_f}{a_5 + d_f + t_f + n_f} \, (dG_f) + \frac{d_n}{c_n + d_n + b_n} \, (dG_n), \tag{4.121}$$

which results in a reserve deficiency equal to

$$R \ def \ 1 = (1 - r) \, d(D + T). \tag{4.122}$$

The banks are now forced to reduce their asset holdings in an amount equal to the reserve deficiency. Thus,

$$R \ def \ 1 = dC_{b1} + dG_{b1} + dF_{b1}. \tag{4.123}$$

Once again, the nonbank-private sectors must be induced to expand their holdings of G and F. (It is assumed that, in this case, the government will not buy any of its securities from the banks.) Offsetting reductions in these sectors' holdings of C, D, and T must result. We have, then,

$$dG_{b1} = dG_{p1} + dG_{f1} + dG_{n1} \tag{4.124}$$

$$dF_{b1} = dF_{p1} + dF_{n1}, \tag{4.125}$$

where

$$dG_{p1} = \frac{g}{g + g_f + g_n} \, dG_{b1} \tag{4.126}$$

$$dG_{f1} = \frac{g_f}{g + g_f + g_n} \, dG_{b1} \tag{4.127}$$

$$dG_{n1} = \frac{g_n}{g + g_f + g_n} \, dG_{b1} \tag{4.128}$$

$$dF_{p1} = \frac{f}{f + b_n} \, dF_{b1} \tag{4.129}$$

$$dF_{n1} = \frac{b_n}{f + b_n} \, dF_{b1}. \tag{4.130}$$

The resultant decreases in assets of the nonbank-private sectors are given by

$$dC_{p1} = \frac{k_2}{k_1 + k_2 + k_3 + n_p} \, (dG_{p1} + dF_{p1}) \tag{4.131}$$

$$dD_{p1} = \frac{k_1}{k_1 + k_2 + k_3 + n_p} \, (dG_{p1} + dF_{p1}) \tag{4.132}$$

$$dT_{p1} = \frac{k_3}{k_1 + k_2 + k_3 + n_p} \, (dG_{p1} + dF_{p1}) \tag{4.133}$$

$$dN_{p1} = \frac{n_p}{k_1 + k_2 + k_3 + n_p} \, (dG_{p1} + dF_{p1}) \tag{4.134}$$

$$dC_{f1} = \frac{a_5}{a_5 + d_f + t_f + n_f} \, dG_{f1} \tag{4.135}$$

$$dD_{f1} = \frac{d_f}{a_5 + d_f + t_f + n_f} \, dG_{f1} \tag{4.136}$$

$$dN_{f1} = \frac{n_f}{a_5 + d_f + t_f + n_f} \, dG_{f1} \tag{4.137}$$

$$dT_{f1} = \frac{t_f}{a_5 + d_f + t_f + n_f} \, dG_{f1} \tag{4.138}$$

$$dC_{n1} = \frac{c_n}{c_n + d_n} \, (dG_{n1} + dF_{n1}) \tag{4.139}$$

$$dD_{n1} = \frac{d_n}{c_n + d_n} \, (dG_{n1} + dF_{n1}). \tag{4.140}$$

These asset readjustments result in a second reserve deficiency, R def 2, given by

$$R \text{ def } 2 = (1 - r) \left[\frac{(k_1 + k_3)}{k_1 + k_2 + k_3 + n_p} (dG_{pl} + dF_{pl}) + \right.$$

$$\left. \frac{d_f + t_f}{a_5 + d_f + n_f + t_f} (dG_{fl}) + \frac{d_n}{c_n + d_n} (dG_{nl} + dF_{nl}) \right]. \quad (4.141)$$

As in the first section of this chapter the banks' reduction of their asset holdings for any particular stage of the process can be written as

$$dG_{bi} = \frac{\rho}{\rho + \gamma + \mu} R \text{ def } i - 1 \qquad (4.142)$$

$$dC_{bi} = \frac{\gamma}{\rho + \gamma + \mu} R \text{ def } i - 1 \qquad (4.143)$$

$$dF_{bi} = \frac{\mu}{\rho + \gamma + \mu} R \text{ def } i - 1. \qquad (4.144)$$

The problem can again be reduced to finding the general term in the infinite series $\sum_{i=1}^{\infty}$ (R def i) and then finding the limit to which this series converges. The expressions for R def 1 and R def 2 are not comparable because of differences in the constant and variable terms in each. It is necessary therefore to examine some of the higher order reserve deficiencies. The general expression for these terms is

$$R \text{ def } j = (1 - r) \left[\frac{k_1 + k_3}{k_1 + k_2 + k_3 + n_p} (dG_{pj-1} + dF_{pj-1}) \right.$$

$$+ \frac{d_f + t_f}{a_5 + d_f + n_f + t_f} (dG_{fj-1}) + \frac{d_n}{c_n + d_n}$$

$$\left. (dG_{nj-1} + dF_{nj-1}) \right] \qquad (4.145)$$

for $j \geq 3$. The expressions for the dG and dF can be written as

$$dG_{pi} = \left(\frac{g}{g + g_f + g_n} \right) \left(\frac{\rho}{\rho + \gamma + \mu} \right) R \text{ def } i - 1$$

$$dG_{fi} = (\frac{g_f}{g + g_f + g_n})(\frac{\rho}{\rho + \gamma + \mu}) \text{ R def i} - 1$$

$$dG_{ni} = (\frac{g_n}{g + g_f + g_n})(\frac{\rho}{\rho + \gamma + \mu}) \text{ R def i} - 1$$

$$dF_{pi} = (\frac{f}{f + b_n})(\frac{\mu}{\rho + \gamma + \mu}) \text{ R def i} - 1$$

$$dF_{ni} = (\frac{b_n}{f + b_n})(\frac{\mu}{\rho + \gamma + \mu}) \text{ R def i} - 1.$$

Substituting these expressions into 4.145 we obtain an expression for R def j in terms of R def j − 1:

$$\text{R def j} = (1 - r)(\frac{k_1 + k_3}{k_1 + k_2 + k_3 + n_p}) \text{ R def j} - 1$$

$$[(\frac{g}{g + g_f + g_n})(\frac{\rho}{\rho + \gamma + \mu}) + (\frac{f}{f + b_n})$$

$$(\frac{\mu}{\rho + \gamma + \mu})] + (1 - r)(\frac{d_f + t_f}{a_5 + d_f + n_f + t_f})$$

$$\text{R def j} - 1[(\frac{g_f}{g + g_f + g_n})(\frac{\rho}{\rho + \gamma + \mu})] +$$

$$(1 - r)\frac{d_n}{c_n + d_n} \text{ R def j} - 1[(\frac{g_n}{g + g_f + g_n})$$

$$(\frac{\rho}{\rho + \gamma + \mu}) + (\frac{b_n}{f + b_n})(\frac{\mu}{\rho + \gamma + \mu})]. \qquad (4.146)$$

Dividing through by R def j − 1,

$$\frac{\text{R def j}}{\text{R def j} - 1} = Q_{G*} = (1 - r)\left\{\frac{k_1 + k_3}{k_1 + k_2 + k_3 + n_p}\right.$$

$$[(\frac{g}{g + g_f + g_n})(\frac{\rho}{\rho + \gamma + \mu}) + (\frac{f}{f + b_n})$$

$$(\frac{\mu}{\rho + \gamma + \mu})] + \frac{d_f + t_f}{a_5 + d_f + n_f + t_f}$$

$$[(\frac{g_f}{g + g_f + g_n}) (\frac{\rho}{\rho + \gamma + \mu})] + \frac{d_n}{c_n + d_n}$$

$$[(\frac{g_n}{g + g_f + g_n}) (\frac{\rho}{\rho + \gamma + \mu}) + (\frac{b_n}{f + b_n})$$

$$(\frac{\mu}{\rho + \gamma + \mu})] \Big\} . \tag{4.147}$$

Equation 4.147 holds for all $j \geq 3$. Consequently,

$$\frac{R \text{ def } 3}{R \text{ def } 2} = Q_{G*} \Rightarrow R \text{ def } 3 = Q_{G*} \, R \text{ def } 2$$

$$\frac{R \text{ def } 4}{R \text{ def } 3} = Q_{G*} \Rightarrow R \text{ def } 4 = Q_{G*} \, R \text{ def } 2$$

.

.

.

$$\frac{R \text{ def } i}{R \text{ def } i - 1} = Q_{G*} \Rightarrow R \text{ def } i = Q_{G*}^{i-2} \, R \text{ def } 2. \tag{4.148}$$

The total reserve deficiency is therefore given by

$$R \text{ def } T = R \text{ def } 1 + R \text{ def } 2 + \sum_{i=3}^{\infty} R \text{ def } i$$

$$= R \text{ def } 1 + R \text{ def } 2 + \sum_{i=3}^{\infty} Q_{G*}^{i-2} R \text{ def } 2.$$

As seen earlier, this infinite series converges to $R \text{ def } 2/1 - Q_{G*}$ since $0 < Q_{G*} < 1$. The total reserve deficiency is therefore

$$R \text{ def } T = R \text{ def } 1 + R \text{ def } 2 + \frac{R \text{ def } 2}{1 - Q_{G*}}$$

$$= \text{R def 1} + \text{R def 2} \left[1 + \frac{1}{1 - Q_{G*}} \right]. \qquad (4.149)$$

Once again, this expression will not be written out in full.

Having obtained the expression for R def T, we are once again in a position to write out the total impacts on asset holdings of the government's role of G* dollars worth of government securities. For the banks, we have:

$$dC_{b:} = \frac{\gamma}{\rho + \gamma + \mu} \text{ R def T} \qquad (4.150)$$

$$dG_{bt} = \frac{\rho}{\rho + \gamma + \mu} \text{ R def T} + \frac{\rho}{\rho + g + g_f + g_n} \text{ G*} \qquad (4.151)$$

$$dF_{bt} = \frac{\mu}{\rho + \gamma + \mu} \text{ R def T}. \qquad (4.152)$$

The nonbank-private sectors have increased their holdings of government and firms' securities by

$$dG_{pt} = \frac{g}{g + g + g} \left[\frac{\rho}{\rho + \gamma + \mu} \text{ R def T} + \right.$$
$$\left. \frac{\rho}{\rho + g + g_f + g_n} \text{ G*} \right] + \frac{g}{\rho + g + g_f + g_n} \text{ G*} \qquad (4.153)$$

$$dG_{nt} = \frac{g_n}{g + g_f + g_n} \left[\frac{\rho}{\rho + \gamma + \mu} \text{ R def T} + \right.$$
$$\left. \frac{\rho}{\rho + g + g_f + g_n} \text{ G*} \right] + \frac{g_n}{\rho + g + g_f + g_n} \text{ G*} \qquad (4.154)$$

$$dG_{ft} = \frac{g_f}{g + g_f + g_n} \left[\frac{\rho}{\rho + \gamma + \mu} \text{ R def T} + \right.$$
$$\left. \frac{\rho}{\rho + g + g_f + g_n} \text{ G*} \right] + \frac{g_f}{\rho + g + g_f + g_n} \text{ G*} \qquad (4.155)$$

$$dF_{pt} = \frac{f}{f + b_n} \; [\frac{\mu}{\rho + \gamma + \mu} \; R \; def \; T] \qquad (4.156)$$

$$dF_{nt} = \frac{b_n}{f + b_n} \; [\frac{\mu}{\rho + \gamma + \mu} \; R \; def \; T]. \qquad (4.157)$$

Summing over each sector,

$$d(G_p + F_p)_t = \frac{g}{g + g_f + g_n} \; [\frac{\rho}{\rho + \gamma + \mu} \; R \; def \; T +$$

$$\frac{\rho}{\rho + g + g_f + g_n} \; G*] + \frac{g}{\rho + g + g_f + g_n} \; G*$$

$$+ \frac{f}{f + b_n} \; [\frac{\mu}{\rho + \gamma + \mu} \; R \; def \; T] \qquad (4.158)$$

$$d(G_n + F_n)_t = \frac{g_n}{g + g_f + g_n} \; [\frac{\rho}{\rho + \gamma + \mu} \; R \; def \; T +$$

$$\frac{\rho}{\rho + g + g_f + g_n} \; G*] + \frac{g_n}{\rho + g + g_f + g_n} \; G*$$

$$+ \frac{b_n}{f + b_n} \; [\frac{\mu}{\rho + \gamma + \mu} \; R \; def \; T]. \qquad (4.159)$$

$$dG_{ft} = 4.155.$$

The resulting decreases in nonbank-private sectors' asset holdings are given by the same relations as 4.73 through 4.82 and will not be repeated here, even though the expressions for $d(G + F)_{pt}$ and $d(G + F)_{nt}$ are not the same as in the first section of this chapter.

The total change in the money stock, dM_{tG*}, is given by

$$dM_{tG*} = \frac{k_2 + k_1}{k_1 + k_2 + k_3 + np} \; d(G + F)_{pt} + d(G + F)_{nt}$$

$$+ \frac{a_5 + d_f}{a_5 + d_f + n_f + t_f} dG_f + \frac{\gamma}{\rho + \gamma + \mu}$$

$$[\text{R def T}] + \frac{\gamma}{\gamma + \mu} G^*. \tag{4.160}$$

All the terms here are the same as those in 4.87 with the exception of $(\gamma/\gamma + \mu)$ G^*, which represents the portion of the banks' initial purchases of government securities paid for by drawing down the banks' currency balances. In the case under discussion dM_{tG^*} is, of course, negative. The same arguments hold for the situation in which the government buys securities. Only the signs need be changed to protect the innocent; otherwise, the relations are identical to those above.

We turn now to consider the effects of open-market operations on the prices of securities (on the rates of interest). In the case under discussion, prices must be lowered (rates increased) on government and firms' securities to induce the nonbank-private sectors to expand their holdings of these securities. The aggregate demands are

$$G_a^D = gY + A_{26}\bar{r}_p + g_nN + A_{15}\bar{r}_n + g_f(PX) + A_7\bar{r}_f \tag{4.161}$$

$$F_a^D = b_nN + A_{17}\bar{r}_n + n_pY + A_{30}\bar{r}_p. \tag{4.162}$$

We have omitted the banks' demand for government and firms' securities, since the new price must induce the nonbank-private sectors to absorb the appropriate amount of securities, e.g., $dG_{pt} + dG_{nt} + dG_{ft}$, and $dF_{pt} + dF_{nt}$. Revisiting 4.161 and 4.162 in terms of only the variables directly affected by open-market operations:

$$G_a^D = A_{26}\bar{r}_p + g_nN + A_{15}\bar{r}_n + A_7\bar{r}_f$$

$$F_a^D = b_nN + A_{17}\bar{r}_n + A_{30}\bar{r}_p.$$

Then it must be true that

$$dG_a^D = dG_{pt} + dG_{nt} + dG_{ft} = A_{26}d\bar{r}_p + g_ndN + A_7d\bar{r}_f + A_{15}\bar{r}_n$$

$$dF_a^D = dF_{pt} + dF_{nt} = b_ndN + A_{17}d\bar{r}_n + A_{30}d\bar{r}_p.$$

We know that

$$dG_{pt} + dG_{nt} + dG_{ft} = \frac{\rho}{\rho + \gamma + \mu} R \text{ def } T + \frac{\rho}{\rho + g + g_f + g_n} G^*$$

$$+ \frac{g + g_f + g_n}{\rho + g + g_f + g_n} G^* = \frac{\rho}{\rho + \gamma + \mu} R \text{ def } T + G^*$$

and that

$$dF_{pt} + dF_{nt} = \frac{\mu}{\rho + \gamma + \mu} R \text{ def } T,$$

so that

$$\frac{\rho}{\rho + \gamma + \mu} R \text{ def } T + G^* = A_{26} d\bar{r}_p + g_n dN + A_{15} \bar{r}_n$$

$$+ A_7 d\bar{r}_f \tag{4.163}$$

and

$$\frac{\mu}{\rho + \gamma + \mu} R \text{ def } T = b_n dN + A_{17} d\bar{r}_n + A_{30} d\bar{r}_p \tag{4.164}$$

or

$$\frac{\rho}{\rho + \gamma + \mu} R \text{ def } T + G^* = (a_7 + a_{15} + a_{26}) dr_f +$$

$$(b_7 + b_{15} + b_{26}) dr_g \tag{4.165}$$

and

$$\frac{\mu}{\rho + \gamma + \mu} R \text{ def } T = b_n dN + (a_{17} + a_{30}) dr_f +$$

$$(b_{17} + b_{30}) dr_g. \tag{4.166}$$

Solving 4.165 and 4.166 simultaneously yields the changes in the rates of interest $(1/dP)$ necessary to induce the increased holdings of G and F in terms of R def T, dN, and G*.

The resulting expressions for dr_f and dr_g are quite similar to those derived in the first section, except for the addition of the term G*:

$$dr_{gG*} = R \text{ def } T \left[\frac{\rho}{\rho + \gamma + \mu} - \frac{a_7 + a_{15} + a_{26}}{a_{17} + a_{30}} \right.$$

$$\left(\frac{\mu}{\rho + \gamma + \mu} \right)] + dN \left[\frac{ \left[(\frac{a_7 + a_{15} + a_{26}}{a_{17} + a_{30}}) b_n - g_n \right] }{ b_7 + b_{15} + b_{26} - (\frac{a_7 + a_{15} + a_{26}}{a_{17} + a_{30}})(b_{17} + b_{30}) } \right] \qquad (4.167)$$

$$dr_{fG*} = \frac{R \text{ def } T}{a_{17} + a_{30}} \left\{ \frac{\mu}{\rho + \gamma + \mu} - (b_{17} + b_{30}) \right.$$

$$\left[\frac{ \frac{\rho}{\rho + \gamma + \mu} - \frac{(a_7 + a_{15} + a_{26})}{(a_{17} + a_{30})} (\frac{\mu}{\rho + \gamma + \mu}) }{ b_7 + b_{15} + b_{26} - (b_{17} + b_{30}) } \right] \right\}$$

$$- \frac{dN}{a_{17} + a_{30}} \left\{ b_n + (b_{17} + b_{30}) \right.$$

$$\left[\frac{ b_n \frac{(a_7 + a_{15} + a_{26})}{a_{17} + a_{30}} - g_n }{ b_7 + b_{15} + b_{26} - (b_{17} + b_{30}) } \right] \right\} +$$

$$\frac{(b_{17} + b_{30})G*}{(a_{17} + a_{30}) [b_7 + b_{15} + b_{26} - (b_{17} + b_{30})]} . \qquad (4.168)$$

As in the first section of this chapter, the expressions for dM_{tG*}, dr_{gG*}, and dr_{fG*} enable us to calculate the other effects of open-market operations on the economy when combined with the various rates of change calculated in chapter 3. These other effects will now be examined for the three tools of monetary policy.

The Effects and Effectiveness
of the Tools of Monetary Policy

In the first three sections of this chapter were developed, with some rigor, expressions for the effects of the various tools of monetary policy on the money stock, the rate on government securities, and the rate on firms' securities. In this section the primary goal is to compare the effects of these tools and their effectiveness in combatting inflation and unemployment.

First, as far as the effects of these tools are concerned, it is clear that changes in the rediscount rate affect the economy through different channels than those through which changes in both the reserve requirement and open-market operations work. Changes in the rediscount rate work primarily (when they have any impact at all) through their impact on the amount of loans actually made by the banking system. Changes in the amount of loans in turn affect the rates charged by the banks as well as the aggregate demand for both consumer and capital goods. Changes in the money stock are not an important channel through which the rediscount rate affects the economy. On the other hand, changes in both the reserve requirement and open-market operations have as their prime avenues of influence changes in the money stock and in the rates on government and firms' securities.

Second, while their effects are very similar, changes in the reserve requirement have one direct effect not shared by open-market operations. Changes in r affect the amount the bank is willing to lend per dollar of deposits as well as the total amount of loans supplied through changes in the amount of deposits. Open-market operations do not affect the quantity of loans supplied per dollar of deposits except insofar as changes in rates of interest resulting from open-market operations may change this figure. (This indirect effect is also shared by changes in reserve requirements.) Thus, given a particular change in the reserve requirement and an open-market operation that both cause the same change in banks' reserves, the change in r results in a greater change in the quantity of bank loans supplied than does the open-market operation.

Third, an open-market operation results in both buying and selling of government securities by the banking system, while the banks either only buy or only sell government securities given a change in r. This difference is of little importance.

A direct comparison of open-market operations and changes in reserve requirements based on the relations developed in the first and third sections of this chapter will now be considered. The analysis will be divided into two major parts. Given a dr and G^* that produce equal changes in the banks' reserves, what are the relationships between the resultant changes in the money stock, r_g, and r_f? What combinations of dr and G^* cause an equal change in the banks' reserves?

The impacts of dr and G^* on M, r_f, and r_g are:

$$dM_{tr} = \frac{\gamma}{\rho + \gamma + \mu} \ R \ \text{def} \ T + [\ \frac{k_2 + k_1}{k_1 + k_2 + k_3 + n_p} \ ] \ d(G + F)_{pt}$$

$$+ \ d(G + F)_{nt} + \frac{a_5 + d_f}{a_5 + d_f + n_f + t_f} \ dG_{ft} \qquad (4.87)$$

$$dr_{gr} = R \ \text{def} \ T \ [\ \frac{\rho}{\rho + \gamma + \mu} \ - \ \frac{a_7 + a_{15} + a_{26}}{a_{17} + a_{30}} \ (\ \frac{\mu}{\rho + \gamma + \mu})]$$

$$\frac{+ \ dN \ [b_n \ \dfrac{a_7 + a_{15} + a_{26}}{a_{17} + a_{30}} \ - \ g_n]}{b_7 + b_{15} + b_{26} \ - \ \dfrac{a_7 + a_{15} + a_{26}}{a_{17} + a_{30}} \ (b_{17} + b_{30})} \qquad (4.94)$$

$$dr_{fr} = \frac{R \ \text{def} \ T}{a_{17} + a_{30}} \ \left\{ \frac{\mu}{\rho + \gamma + \mu} \ - \ (b_{17} + b_{30}) \right.$$

$$[\ \frac{\dfrac{\rho}{\rho + \gamma + \mu} \ - \ \dfrac{(a_7 + a_{15} + a_{26})}{a_{17} + a_{30}} \ (\dfrac{\mu}{\rho + \gamma + \mu})}{b_7 + b_{15} + b_{26} \ - \ (b_{17} + b_{30})} \ ] \left. \right\} \ - \ \frac{dN}{a_{17} + a_{30}}$$

$$\left\{ b_n \ - \ (b_{17} + b_{30}) \ [\ \frac{\dfrac{b_n(a_7 + a_{15} + a_{26})}{a_{17} + a_{30}} \ - \ g_n}{b_7 + b_{15} + b_{26} \ - \ (b_{17} + b_{30})} \ ] \right\} \qquad (4.95)$$

$$dM_{tG^*} = \frac{k_2 + k_1}{k_1 + k_2 + k_3 + n_p} \ d(G + F)_{pt} + d(G + F)_{nt} +$$

$$\frac{a_5 + d_f}{a_5 + d_f + n_f + t_f}\ dG_f + \frac{\gamma}{\rho + \gamma + \mu}\ [R\ def\ T]\ +$$

$$\frac{\gamma}{\gamma + \mu}\ G^* \tag{4.160}$$

$$dr_{gG^*} = R\ def\ T\ [\frac{\rho}{\rho + \gamma + \mu} - \frac{a_7 + a_{15} + a_{26}}{a_{17} + a_{30}}$$

$$(\frac{\mu}{\rho + \gamma + \mu})] + dN\ [(\frac{a_7 + a_{15} + a_{26}}{a_{17} + a_{30}})$$

$$\frac{b_n - g_n + G^*]}{b_7 + b_{15} + b_{26} - (\frac{a_7 + a_{15} + a_{26}}{a_{17} + a_{30}})(b_{17} + b_{30})} \tag{4.167}$$

$$dr_{fG^*} = \frac{R\ def\ T}{a_{17} + a_{30}}\ \left\{ \frac{\mu}{\rho + \gamma + \mu} - (b_{17} + b_{30}) \right.$$

$$[\frac{\frac{\rho}{\rho + \gamma + \mu} - \frac{(a_7 + a_{15} + a_{26})}{(a_{17} + a_{30})}(\frac{\mu}{\rho + \gamma + \mu})}{b_7 + b_{15} + b_{26} - (b_{17} + b_{30})}]\left.\right\}$$

$$- \frac{dN}{a_{17} + a_{30}}\ \left\{ b_n + (b_{17} + b_{30}) \right.$$

$$[\frac{\frac{b_n(a_7 + a_{15} + a_{26})}{a_{17} + a_{30}} - g_n}{b_7 + b_{15} + b_{26} - (b_{17} + b_{30})}]\left.\right\}\ +$$

$$\frac{(b_{17} + b_{30})G^*}{(a_{17} + a_{30})\ [b_7 + b_{15} + b_{26} - (b_{17} + b_{30})]}\ . \tag{4.168}$$

Comparison of dM_{tG^*} and dM_{tr} shows the two expressions to be (superficially) identical with the exception of the term $(\gamma/\gamma + \mu)\ G^*$ in dM_{tG^*}. This term is the banks' initial changes in currency holdings as a result of first purchase or sale of government securities. If it is sure that equal changes in reserves imply equal changes in the nonbank-private sectors' holdings of government and firms' securities, then it would seem that, even though G^* and dr resulted in an equal change in reserves, G^*

had a greater impact on the money stock. To be sure of this conclusion, the relations between the terms $d(G + F)_{pt}$, $d(G + F)_{nt}$, and dG_f in the two equations must be examined. These terms are given by

$$d(G + F)_{ptG*} = \frac{g}{g + g_f + g_n} \left[\frac{\rho}{\rho + \gamma + \mu} R \text{ def } T + \right.$$

$$\frac{\rho}{\rho + g + g_f + g_n} G*] + \frac{g}{\rho + g + g_f + g_n} G*$$

$$+ \frac{f}{f + b_n} \left[\frac{\mu}{\rho + \gamma + \mu} R \text{ def } T \right] \tag{4.158}$$

$$d(G + F)_{ntG*} = \frac{g_n}{g + g_f + g_n} \left[\frac{\rho}{\rho + \gamma + \mu} R \text{ def } T + \right.$$

$$\frac{\rho}{\rho + g + g_f + g_n} G*] + \frac{g_n}{\rho + g + g_f + g_n} G*$$

$$+ \frac{b_n}{f + b_n} \left[\frac{\mu}{\rho + \gamma + \mu} R \text{ def } T \right] \tag{4.159}$$

$$dG_{gtG*} = \frac{g_f}{g + g_f + g_n} \left[\frac{\rho}{\rho + \gamma + \mu} R \text{ def } T + \right.$$

$$\frac{\rho}{\rho + g + g_f + g_n} G*] + \frac{g_{nf}}{\rho + g + g_f + g_n} G* \tag{4.155}$$

$$d(G + F)_{ptr} = \frac{g}{g + g_f + g_n} \left(\frac{\rho}{\rho + \gamma + \mu} R \text{ def } T - dG_{go} \right)$$

$$+ \frac{f}{f + b_n} \left(\frac{\mu}{\rho + \gamma + \mu} R \text{ def } T \right) \tag{4.71}$$

$$d(G + F)_{ntr} = \frac{g_n}{g + g_f + g_n} \left(\frac{\rho}{\rho + \gamma + \mu} R \text{ def } T - dG_{go} \right)$$

$$+ \frac{b_n}{f + b_n} \left(\frac{\mu}{\rho + \gamma + \mu} R \text{ def } T \right) \tag{4.72}$$

$$dG_{ftr} = \frac{g_f}{g + g_f + g_n} \left(\frac{\rho}{\rho + \gamma + \mu} \ R \ def \ T - dG_{go} \right). \qquad (4.68)$$

Comparison of these terms shows unambiguously that $d(G + F)_{ptG*}$ $> d(G + F)_{ptr}$, $d(G + F)_{ntG*} > d(G + F)_{ntr}$, and $dG_{ftG*} > dG_{ftr}$. This is not surprising, as one of the chief characteristics of open-market operations is that they change the total amount of government securities held by the private sectors, while changing r does not have this effect (except to the extent the government decides as a matter of policy either to buy or sell government securities in conjunction with the change in r). Consequently, it can be concluded unambiguously that, when $G*$ and dr result in the same change in banks' reserves, the impact of $G*$ on the money stock will be larger than that of dr. Furthermore, comparison of the expressions for dr_f and dr_g also shows that $dr_{gG*} >$ dr_{gr} and $dr_{fG*} > dr_{fr}$. Thus, it can be concluded that, even though both dr and $G*$ result in the same change in reserves of the banking system, $G*$ (an open-market operation) will have a greater impact on the level of economic activity since $G*$ results in greater changes in M, r_f, and r_g than does dr.[3]

The next question is what combination of dr and $G*$ results in an equal change in banks' reserves? The expressions for the total change in banks' reserves are

$$R \ def \ T_r = R \ def \ 1_r + R \ def \ 2_r + R \ def \ 3_r \left(1 + \frac{1}{1 - Q_r}\right) \qquad (4.158)$$

$$R \ def \ T_{G*} = R \ def \ 1_{G*} + R \ def \ 2_{G*} \left[1 + \frac{1}{1 - Q_{G*}}\right] \qquad (4.149)$$

where

$$Q_r = Q_{G*} - dr,$$

3. It is not meant to stress these differences between changes in the reserve requirements and open-market operations at the expense of institutional differences which the model does not take into account. Some of these differences are the fact that open-market operations work slowly, relative to changes in reserve requirements, the possibility that bankers view reserves created by changes in reserve requirements differently than reserves generated by open-market operations, etc.

so that when $dr < 0$,

$$(1 + \frac{1}{1 - Q_r}) > (1 + \frac{1}{1 - Q_{G*}})$$

and vice versa when $dr > 0$.

Rather than base this analysis on a complete investigation of R def T_r and R def T_{G*}, we assume that an accurate approximation of the answer can be found in a comparison of the first changes in the banks' reserves.

$$\text{R def } 1_r = dr(D + T)$$

$$\text{R def } 1_{G*} = (1 - r) \left[\left(\frac{k_1 + k_3}{k_1 + k_2 + k_3 + n_p} \right) \left(\frac{g}{\rho + g + g_f + g_n} \right) G* \right.$$

$$+ \left(\frac{d_f + t_f}{a_5 + d_f + n_f + t_f} \right) \left(\frac{g_f}{\rho + g + g_f + g_n} \right) G* +$$

$$\left. \left(\frac{d_n}{c_n + d_n + b_n} \right) \left(\frac{g_n}{\rho + g + g_f + g_n} \right) G* \right].$$

Thus, for R def 1_r to equal R def 1_{G*}, it must be true that

$$\frac{G*}{dr} = \frac{D + T}{(1-r) \left[\left(\frac{k_1 + k_3}{k_1 + k_2 + k_3 + n_p} \right) \left(\frac{g}{\rho + g + g_f + g_n} \right) + \left(\frac{d_f + t_f}{a_5 + d_f + n_f + t_f} \right) \left(\frac{g_f}{\rho + g + g_f + g_n} \right) + \left(\frac{d_n}{c_n + d_n + b_n} \right) \left(\frac{g_n}{\rho + g + g_f + g_n} \right) \right]}. \tag{4.169}$$

The denominator of 4.169 is clearly less than 1. Call it dem. Then, to produce the same first change in reserves as a 1 percentage point change in r, open-market operations in an amount equal to

$$\frac{G*}{.01} = (D + T) \frac{1}{\text{dem}} \text{ or } G* = .01(D + T) \frac{1}{\text{dem}} \tag{4.170}$$

must be undertaken. The exact size of this G* depends, of course, on the sizes of the parameters in the denominator of 4.169 and on the size of D + T. Even though it is recognized that only looking at the first reserve change probably provides an inaccurate answer to the question, 4.170 certainly underscores the strength of changes in the reserve requirement as a monetary tool when one considers the size of G* necessary to produce the same first change in reserves as a 1 percentage point change in r.

We conclude this comparison of changes in r and open-market operations by noting that an open-market operation smaller than the G* in 4.170 will produce the same change in the money stock and in the rates on securities as does a 1 percentage point change in r. This is obvious since we have already shown that a G* which causes the same total change in reserves as a particular dr will have a greater impact on M, r_f, and r_g than the change in the reserve requirement. This observation also underscores the strength of dr, since a G* of substantial size would have to be undertaken to produce equivalent changes in M, r_f, and r_g.

We turn now to a consideration of the effectiveness of these tools of monetary policy in combatting the problems of inflation and unemployment. With regard to changes in the rediscount rate, Table 10 shows that the only circumstances in which it has any impact on the economy are when there is an excess demand for bank loans. Typically, excess demand situations would correspond to periods of inflation, while one of the characteristics of unemployment would be an excess supply of bank loans. Thus, we can conclude that changes in the rediscount rate will be particularly ineffective in combatting unemployment. The effectiveness of this tool is limited to combatting inflation. Even here, the impact of any changes in r_d is likely to be small.

This asymmetry of the effects of changes in the rediscount rate is not shared by changes in the reserve requirement and open-market operations. As indicated, the arguments presented, though framed in terms of reductions in total reserves, hold equally well for changes in r and open-market operations aimed at increasing the reserves of the banking system. Thus, there is little to choose between changes in reserve requirements and open-market operations when one is faced by either unemployment or inflation.[4] The equations below measure the impact of changes in r and open-market operations on the variables of the

___

4. Except institutional factors which, it has been argued, prevent fractional and frequent changes in the reserve requirement. These arguments have no economic validity, but are probably valid from other points of view.

economy, and illustrate the channels through which these tools operate in achieving their results.

The immediate impact on Y as a result of either dr or G* is the sum of three effects: the impact on Y of the change in the money stock resulting from dr or G*; the impact on Y of the change in r_f resulting from either dr or G*; and the impact on Y of the change in r_g resulting from either dr or G*. Thus,

$$dY_r = \frac{\partial Y}{\partial M} dM_r + \frac{\partial Y}{\partial r_f} dr_{fr} + \frac{\partial Y}{\partial r_g} dr_{gr} \qquad (4.171)$$

$$dY_{G*} = \frac{\partial Y}{\partial M} dM_{G*} + \frac{\partial Y}{\partial r_f} dr_{fG*} + \frac{\partial Y}{\partial r_g} dr_{gG*}. \qquad (4.172)$$

Similar expressions can be written out for the effects on X_c, X_k, P_c, and P_k:

$$dX_{c(k)r(G*)} = \frac{\partial X_{c(k)}}{\partial M} dM_{r(G*)} + \frac{\partial X_{c(k)}}{\partial r_f} dr_{fr(G*)} +$$

$$\frac{\partial X_{c(k)}}{\partial r_g} dr_{g(G*)} \qquad (4.173)$$

$$dP_{c(k)r(G*)} = \frac{\partial P_{c(k)}}{\partial M} dM_{r(G*)} + \frac{\partial P_{c(k)}}{\partial r_f} dr_{f(G*)} +$$

$$\frac{\partial P_{c(k)}}{\partial r_g} dr_{gr(G*)}, \qquad (4.174)$$

where the terms in the parentheses are used to indicate the other variables for which separate equations could be written. Equations 4.173 and 4.174 actually represent eight different expressions.

Rather than reproduce the explicit forms of all the relations 4.171 through 4.174, we will present only one, that for 4.171, as an illustration.

$$dY_r = [\frac{\partial X_c}{\partial M} P_c + \frac{\partial P_c}{\partial M} X_c + \frac{\partial X_k}{\partial M} P_k + \frac{\partial P_k}{\partial M} X_k + \frac{\partial \pi_b}{\partial M} + \frac{\partial \pi_n}{\partial M}$$

$$+ r_g \frac{\partial G_p}{\partial M} + \frac{\partial r_g}{\partial M} G_p + \frac{\partial r_t}{\partial M} T_p + \frac{\partial T_p}{\partial M} r_t + \frac{\partial r_n}{\partial M} N_p + \frac{\partial N_p}{\partial M}$$

$$r_n + \frac{\partial r_f}{\partial M} F_p + \frac{\partial F_p}{\partial M} r_f - (\frac{\partial r_{bf}}{\partial M} L_{bf} + \frac{\partial L_{bf}}{\partial M} r_{bf} +$$

$$\frac{\partial r_{nf}}{\partial M} L_{nf} + \frac{\partial L_{nf}}{\partial M} r_{nf})] \ [\ \frac{\gamma}{\rho + \gamma + \mu} \ R \ def \ T_r +$$

$$(\frac{k_2 + k_1}{k_1 + k_2 + k_3 + n_p}) \ d(G + F)_{pt} + d(G + F)_{nt} +$$

$$(\frac{a_5 + d_f}{a_5 + d_f + n_f + t_f}) \ dG_{pt}] + [\frac{\partial X_c}{\partial r_f} P_c + \frac{\partial P_c}{\partial r_f} X_c + \frac{\partial X_k}{\partial r_f} P_k$$

$$+ \frac{\partial P_k}{\partial r_f} X_k + \frac{\partial \pi_b}{\partial r_f} + \frac{\partial \pi_n}{\partial r_f} + r_g \frac{\partial G_p}{\partial r_f} + \frac{\partial r_g}{\partial r_f} G_p + \frac{\partial r_t}{\partial r_f} T_p +$$

$$\frac{\partial T_p}{\partial r_f} r_t + \frac{\partial r_n}{\partial r_f} N_p + \frac{\partial N_p}{\partial r_f} r_n + F_p + \frac{\partial F_p}{\partial r_f} r_f - (\frac{\partial r_{bf}}{\partial r_f} L_{bf}$$

$$+ \frac{\partial L_{bf}}{\partial r_f} r_{bf} + \frac{\partial r_{nf}}{\partial r_f} L_{nf} + \frac{\partial L_{nf}}{\partial r_f} r_{nf})] \ [\frac{R \ def \ T_r}{a_{17} + a_{30}}$$

$$\left\{ \frac{\mu}{\rho + \gamma + \mu} - (b_{17} + b_{30}) \right.$$

$$[\frac{\frac{\rho}{\rho + \gamma + \mu} - \frac{(a_7 + a_{15} + a_{26})}{a_{17} + a_{30}} (\frac{\mu}{\rho + \gamma + \mu})}{b_7 + b_{16} + b_{26} - (b_{17} + b_{30})}] -$$

$$\frac{d_n}{a_{17} + a_{30}} \left\{ b_n - (b_{17} + b_{30}) \right\}$$

$$[\frac{\frac{b_n(a_7 + a_{15} + a_{26})}{a_{17} + a_{30}} - g_n}{b_7 + b_{15} + b_{26} - (b_{17} + b_{30})}] \right\} \ ] + [\frac{\partial X_c}{\partial r_g} P_c +$$

$$\frac{\partial P_c}{\partial r_g} X_c + \frac{\partial X_k}{\partial r_g} P_k + \frac{\partial P_k}{\partial r_g} X_k + \frac{\partial \pi_b}{\partial r_g} + G_p + \frac{\partial G_p}{\partial r_g} r_g +$$

$$\frac{\partial r_t}{\partial r_g} T_p + \frac{\partial T_p}{\partial r_g} r_t + \frac{\partial r_n}{\partial r_g} N_p + \frac{\partial N_p}{\partial r_g} r_n + \frac{\partial r_f}{\partial r_g} F_p + \frac{\partial F_p}{\partial r_g} r_f$$

$$- (\frac{\partial r_{bf}}{\partial r_g} L_{bf} + \frac{\partial L_{bf}}{\partial r_g} r_{bf} + \frac{\partial r_{nf}}{\partial r_g} L_{nf} + \frac{\partial L_{nf}}{\partial r_g} r_{nf})]$$

$$R \text{ def } T_r \left\{ \frac{\rho}{\rho + \gamma + \mu} - \frac{(a_7 + a_{15} + a_{26})}{a_{17} + a_{30}} \right.$$

$$\left. (\frac{\mu}{\rho + \gamma + \mu}) \right\} + dN \left\{ b_n (\frac{a_7 + a_{15} + a_{26}}{a_{17} + a_{30}}) \right.$$

$$[\frac{\left. - g_n \right\}}{b_7 + b_{15} + b_{26} - \frac{(a_7 + a_{15} + a_{26})}{a_{17} + a_{30}} (b_{17} + b_{30})}]. \quad (4.175)$$

The complexity of this equation speaks for itself. It clearly illustrates, however, the pervasive influence of the changes in M, r_f, and r_g associated with (in this case) a change in the reserve requirement.

It should be noted at this point that the relations 4.171 through 4.174 actually understate the effects of dr and G* on the pertinent variables in the model. The basic reason for this is that they ignore such things as, for example, the impact on prices and outputs of changes in the other rates of interest (other than r_g and r_f) induced by changes in M, r_f, and r_g. Furthermore, the change in Y itself will induce another round of changes in M and the other variables in the model. These second, third, and higher generation changes are not contained in 4.171 through 4.174. This does not mean that their impacts cannot be measured (although it is a messy job). For example, consider the effects of the original changes in Y, dY_r; r_g, dr_{gr}; and r_f, and dr_{fr} on the money stock. The "second-generation" change in M is given by

$$dM_{r2} = \frac{\partial M}{\partial Y} dY_r + \frac{\partial M}{\partial r_f} dr_{fr} + \frac{\partial M}{\partial r_g} dr_{gr} + \frac{\partial M}{\partial \bar{r}} \frac{\partial \bar{r}}{\partial M} dM_r +$$

$$\frac{\partial M}{\partial \bar{r}} \frac{\partial \bar{r}}{\partial r_f} df_r + \frac{\partial M}{\partial \bar{r}} \frac{\partial \bar{r}}{\partial r_g} dr_{gr} \qquad (4.176)$$

where the last two terms reflect the impact of changes in other rates on M induced by changes in r_g and r_f, while the third from last term captures the effects of changes in M on M. To answer the question of the total size of the second and higher generation effects, one would have to resort again to finding the general terms for several infinite series and then testing these series for convergence. This has not been done, primarily because the model has, I hope, been formulated in such a way that the majority of the impacts on the economy are captured by the relations 4.171 through 4.174.

5. Results of the Study

BY THE TERM "monetary mechanism" I mean the complex web
of causal relations through which interest rates, prices, and real phenomena react to determine the money stock, as well as the chain of
causality running in the opposite direction—the impact of the stock of
money on the real and financial variables of the economy. The model
constructed in chapter 2 enables examination of both of these facets of
the monetary mechanism.

Based on the identity for the money stock (see Equation 3.3) expressions were derived for the rates of change in M with respect to the key
variables of the model. These expressions were of the form

$$\frac{\partial M}{\partial Z} = C_1 \frac{\partial(PX)}{\partial Z} + C_2 \frac{\partial Y}{\partial Z} + C_3 \frac{\partial \bar{r}_f}{\partial Z} + C_4 \frac{\partial \bar{r}_p}{\partial Z} + C_5$$

$$\frac{\partial \bar{r}_n}{\partial Z} \tag{5.1}$$

where Z is any interest rate, price, real output, or income. From 5.1, I
conclude that a change in any of these variables affects the stock of
money through its impact on prices (P), real output (X), income (Y),
and the various rates of interest. The terms C_1 through C_5 are in a sense
"money multipliers." They show by how much the money stock
changes, given a change in the variables with which they are associated.
(See Tables 3–7 and the associated discussion for a complete description
and interpretation of these terms.) I have thus developed a scientific
money multiplier for each of the key variables in the model. The
Brunner-Meltzer and Teigen models develop only a single money multiplier, while the C's are only some of several "multipliers" I have
developed. (Other multipliers include the Q's developed in the analysis
of the effects of changes in reserve requirements and open-market
operations.)

The next step in the analysis of this facet of the monetary mechanism was an exploration of the specific terms on the right-hand side of 5.1. I showed how each of these terms could be derived and upon what variables they depend. The thirteen equations of the form 5.1, coupled with the description of the terms on the right-hand sides of these equations provided in chapter 3, constitute a complete description of the facet of the monetary mechanism where the chain of causality runs from the variables of the economy to the stock of money.

The general equilibrium nature of the approach and the addition of more sectors and variables provide a greater wealth of detail and a more comprehensive description of how the money stock reacts to changes in the economy than any of the other extant studies of the money supply. I have spelled out the specific behavioral functions and built from these, whereas the other studies only indicate somewhat fuzzily upon what variables the terms in their money supply functions depend.[1]

The major advance provided by this portion of the study is the explicit demonstration of the links among the variables in the model and the money stock. I have clearly displayed these links rather than hiding the guts of this portion of the monetary mechanism behind highly simplified identities for the money stock of the sort developed by Friedman and Schwartz, Brunner and Meltzer, and Teigen, or behind a logically inconsistent equation as developed by de Leeuw.

The addition of an examination of the links running from the money stock to the variables of the model represents an important advance over extant studies. Expressions for $\partial Z / \partial M$ have been described and analyzed, where Z again is any variable (price, interest rate, income, output) in the model.[2] This analysis serves the extremely useful purpose of persuading us that a study of the monetary mechanism is important, since changes in M will have an impact on the real and financial variables of the economy. We have shown that the impact of M on real outputs operates through the effects of changes in M on income, prices, and interest rates, thus affecting both the demand and supply of goods. Even if we assume that all demand functions are homogeneous of degree zero in all their arguments (which was not done), a change in the money

---

1. De Leeuw's model is exempt from most of this criticism, since it is a simultaneous model built on specific behavioral equations.
2. One serendipitous feature of the analysis was a different proof of the quantity theory and a demonstration that interest rate effects on demand and supply may weaken the direct relation between money and prices (see chapter 3) and the importance of downward-sloping demand curves for the quantity theory to hold.

stock will result in a shift in demands, since the change in M will not, in general, produce equiproportional changes in the P's, Y's, and r's. The same argument can be made with regard to shifts in supply. Thus, the only circumstances in which the $\partial X/\partial M$'s will be zero is if the shifts in supply and demand exactly balance each other out. There is no reason to suppose that, in general, this will be the case.

THE TOOLS OF MONETARY POLICY

The model was used to analyze the effects and the effectiveness of the major tools of monetary policy—open-market operations, changes in the reserve requirements, and changes in the rediscount rate—in combatting both inflation and unemployment.

Changes in the rediscount rate were found to be almost completely ineffective in combatting problems of unemployment (characterized by an excess supply of bank loans from unborrowed reserves). They were only somewhat effective in helping solve problems of inflation (when there is likely to be an excess demand for bank loans). In these situations changes in the rediscount rate affect the amount of rediscounting and thus the actual amount of loans made by the bank. Changes in the amounts of bank loans made potentially change the demand for the consumer and capital good, thus affecting the level of economic activity. The implication of these conclusions is to cast more doubt on the usefulness of discretionary changes in the rediscount rate as a monetary tool, especially in combatting problems of unemployment.

The effects of open-market operations and changes in the reserve requirement on the variables of the model were a result of their primary effects on the money stock, the rate on government securities, and the rate on firms' securities. Their effectiveness in combatting inflation depends on the size of

$$(\frac{\partial P_k}{\partial M} + \frac{\partial P_c}{\partial M}) \, dM + (\frac{\partial P_k}{\partial r_g} + \frac{\partial P_c}{\partial r_g}) \, dr_g +$$

$$(\frac{\partial P_k}{\partial r_f} + \frac{\partial P_c}{\partial r_f}) \, dr_f. \tag{5.2}$$

Their effectiveness in combatting unemployment depends on the size of

$$(\frac{\partial X_k}{\partial M} + \frac{\partial X_c}{\partial M}) \, dM + (\frac{\partial X_k}{\partial r_g} + \frac{\partial X_c}{\partial r_g}) \, dr_g +$$

$$(\frac{\partial X_k}{\partial r_f} + \frac{\partial X_c}{\partial r_f}) \, dr_f, \tag{5.3}$$

where the differentials refer to the changes in M, r_g, and r_f caused by either of the two monetary tools. The sizes of the partial derivatives are independent of the particular monetary tool used; consequently one tool can attain the same results as the other.

There were two major differences between the two tools. Open-market operations cause an immediate change in the total size of the private sectors' asset portfolio by changing the total amount of government securities held by the private sectors; changes in the reserve requirement, while indirectly changing the size of the private asset portfolio (through its impact on C, D, and T), do not have this direct effect. Second, changes in the reserve requirement change the quantity of bank loans supplied per dollar of deposits, while open-market operations lack this effect. As a result of these major differences I found that, given an open-market operation and a change in the reserve requirement that produce the same total change in the reserves of the banking system, the open-market operation has a greater impact on both the money stock and on the rate on government securities.[3] I also developed a way of finding combinations of open-market operations and changes in the reserve requirement that produce the same change in total reserves. This formulation added to the belief that changes in reserve requirements are an extremely powerful tool of monetary policy because of the very large open-market operation that would have to be undertaken to produce the same effects as the change in the reserve requirement.

SUGGESTED EMPIRICAL TESTING PROCEDURE

Empirical testing of the model and its conclusions will be centered about the estimation of the elements of the vectors A_i, i = 1, 2, . . . , 30 and the other parameters of the model. Once estimates for these param-

---

3. This conclusion on interest rate effects seems to contradict the findings of Ascheim (2). He found that given an equal reduction in demand deposits, a higher reserve requirement would produce a greater increase in interest rates than a restrictive open-market operation. It is not clear that his analysis, framed in terms of equal changes in demand deposits, and ours in terms of equal changes in reserves are directly comparable.

eters are obtained, numerical estimates of the various multipliers can be obtained.

The second level of testing will center about estimation of the accuracy of the rates of change and total changes predicted by the model. How do the predictions "fit" with changes in M and other variables actually observed?

It is felt that regression analysis and one- and two-stage least squares should comprise the bulk of the statistical techniques to be used. The data to which the model will be fit will be those used by the Brookings-SSRC model.

Completion of this portion of the work will provide an empirical judgment of the conclusions of the work which, to this point, are based strictly on theory and a few assumptions about the signs, but not the magnitudes, of the parameters of the model.

Appendix: Definitions

THIS LIST contains the major symbols used in the model and their definitions. Any Greek letter or lower case English letter not listed above (with or without subscripts) represents a parameter in a decision function for a particular sector.

r	=	the reserve requirement on demand and time deposits
r_f	=	the rate of interest on firms' securities
r_g	=	the rate of interest on government securities
r_n	=	the rate of interest on deposits in intermediaries
r_t	=	the rate of interest on time deposits
r_{bf}	=	the rate of interest on bank loans to firms
r_{bp}	=	the rate of interest on bank loans to the public
r_{nf}	=	the rate of interest on intermediary loans to firms
r_{np}	=	the rate of interest on intermediary loans to the public
r_d	=	the rediscount rate
$\bar{r}_g$	=	the coupon rate on government securities
$\bar{r}_f$	=	$(r_f, r_g, r_n, r_t, r_{bf}, 0, r_{nf}, 0)$
$\bar{r}_b$	=	$(r_f, r_g, 0, r_t, r_{bf}, r_{bp}, 0, 0)$
$\bar{r}_n$	=	$(r_f, r_g, r_n, r_t, 0, 0, r_{nf}, r_{np})$
$\bar{r}_p$	=	$(r_f, r_g, r_n, r_t, 0, r_{bp}, 0, r_{np})$
dr	=	a policy determined change in reserve requirements
A_i	=	$(i = 1, 2, \ldots, 30)$ = column vector of constants
		$= (a_i, b_i, c_i, d_i, e_i, f_i, g_i, h_i)$
A_f	=	vector of firms' assets

145

C = currency

D = demand deposits

D_k = stock demand for capital

dK = flow demand for capital

D_ℓ = demand for labor

DA^D = desired distribution of firms' financial assets

DE^D = desired distribution of firms' retained earnings

d = actual amount of rediscounting

d^d = amount of rediscounting demanded

d_o^d = amount of rediscounting demanded to meet public's demand for loans

d_1^d = amount of rediscounting demanded to meet firms' demand for loans

dZ_f = change in asset Z resulting from a change in the banks' holdings of firms' securities

dZ_g = change in asset Z resulting from a change in the banks' holdings of government securities

dZ_{k1} = change in sector k's holdings of asset Z resulting from a change in sector k's holdings of asset 1

dZ_T = total change in asset Z

dZ_{Tr} = total change in asset Z resulting from a change in reserve requirements

dZ_{TG*} = total change in asset Z resulting from an open-market operation

dM_{Tr} = total change in the money stock resulting from a change in reserve requirements

dM_{TG*} = total change in the money stock resulting from an open-market operation

dr_{xr} = change in interest rate r_x resulting from a change in reserve requirements

dr_{xG*} = change in interest rate r_x resulting from an open-market operation

E^a = actual stock of firms' retained earnings

E^d	=	desired stock of firms' retained earnings
F	=	firms' debt instruments (securities)
F^d	=	firms' demand for financing
F^S	=	firms' supply of new securities
G	=	government securities
$G*$	=	an open-market operation
$\bar{G}$	=	face value of government securities held by the private sectors
G^S	=	supply of government securities
G^D	=	demand for government securities
I_g	=	gross investment
I_n	=	net investment
K	=	capital stock
k	=	rate of growth of the capital stock
L	=	amount of labor in the economy
L_c	=	amount of labor used to produce the consumer good
L_k	=	amount of labor used to produce the capital good
L^b	=	total bank loans
L^n	=	total intermediary loans
L_p	=	total loans to the public
L_f	=	total loans to the firms
L_p^b	=	bank loans to the public
L_f^b	=	bank loans to the firms
L_p^n	=	intermediary loans to the public
L_f^n	=	intermediary loans to the firms
L_f^D	=	firms' aggregate demand for loans
L_f^{Db}	=	firms' demand for bank loans
L_f^{Dn}	=	firms' demand for intermediary loans
L_p^D	=	public's aggregate demand for loans
L_p^{Db}	=	public's demand for bank loans

L_p^{Dn}	=	public's demand for intermediary loans
$\bar{L}^{Sb}$	=	banks' loan supply from unborrowed reserves
$\bar{L}_p^{Sb}$	=	amount banks are willing to loan the public from unborrowed reserves
$\bar{L}_f^{Sb}$	=	amount banks are willing to loan the firms from unborrowed reserves
$\bar{L}^{Sn}$	=	aggregate amount intermediaries are willing to lend
$\bar{L}_p^{Sn}$	=	aggregate amount intermediaries are willing to lend the public
$\bar{L}_f^{Sn}$	=	aggregate amount intermediaries are willing to lend the firms
M	=	the money stock
m	=	the number of consumer good firms
N	=	deposits in intermediaries
n	=	the number of capital good firms
P_c	=	the price of the consumer good
P_k	=	the price of the capital
PX	=	$(P_c X_c + P_k X_k)$
Q_{G*}	=	the ratio of successive reserve changes resulting from an open-market operation
Q_r	=	the ratio of successive reserve changes resulting from a change in reserve requirements
R	=	required reserves
R^S	=	secondary reserves
R def	=	reserve deficiency
$R\,def_T$	=	total reserve deficiency
S^k	=	stock supply of capital
S^ℓ	=	supply of labor
s^k	=	flow supply of capital
T	=	time deposits
T_r	=	tax receipts
t	=	marginal rate of taxation
X_c	=	the consumer good

X_k	=	the capital good
X_{kc}	=	amount of the capital good used in the production of the consumer good
X_{kk}	=	amount of the capital good used in the production of capital
Y	=	public's disposable money income
$\bar{Y}$	=	gross money income
Y_b	=	banks' contribution to income
Y_f	=	firms' contribution to income
Y_n	=	intermediaries' contribution to income
Y_g	=	government's contribution to income
α	=	rate of depreciation
α_c, α_k	=	X_k and X_c intercepts of the transformation curve
λ	=	rate of growth of the labor force
$\emptyset$	=	profit expectation function for the firms
π_b	=	total banks' profits
$\pi_{\varrho b}$	=	banks' profit from loans
π_{gb}	=	banks' profit from government securities
π_{fb}	=	banks' profit from firms' securities
π_n	=	total intermediaries' profit
$\pi_{\varrho n}$	=	intermediaries' profit from loans
π_{gn}	=	intermediaries' profit from government securities
π_{fn}	=	intermediaries' profit from firms' securities

Literature Cited

1. Angell, J. *The behavior of money; exploratory studies.* New York: McGraw-Hill Book Co., Inc., 1936.
2. Ascheim, J. Restrictive open market operations versus reserve requirement increases: a reformulation. *Economic Journal* 73 (1963): 254-66.
3. Baumol, W. The transactions demand for cash: an inventory theoretic approach. *Quarterly Journal of Economics* 66 (1952): 545-56.
4. Brunner, K. A schema for the supply theory of money. *International Economic Review* 2 (1961): 77-88.
5. ——— . Some major problems in monetary theory. *American Economic Review* 51 (1961): 381-97.
6. Brunner, K., and Meltzer, A. *An alternative approach to the monetary mechanism.* Washington: U.S. Government Printing Office, 1964.
7. Brunner, K., and Meltzer, A. Predicting velocity: implications for theory and policy. *Journal of Finance* 18 (1963): 319-54.
8. Brunner, K., and Meltzer, A. Some further investigation of the demand and supply functions of money. *Journal of Finance* 19 (1964): 321-59.
9. Cagan, P. The demand for currency relative to the total money supply. *Journal of Political Economy* 66 (1958): 303-28.
10. ——— . *Determinants and effects of changes in the stock of money, 1875-1960.* Washington: National Bureau of Economic Research, 1965.
11. Chase, S., and Gramley, L. Time deposits in monetary analysis. *Federal Reserve Bulletin* 51 (1965): 1380-1406.
12. Curry, L. *The supply and control of money in the United States.* Cambridge: Harvard University Press, 1934.
13. Davidson, Paul. Money, portfolio balance, capital accumulation, and economic growth. *Econometrica* 36 (1968): 291-321.
14. Davidson, Paul, and Smolensky, E. Modigliani on the interaction of real and monetary phenomena. *Review of Economics and Statistics* 46 (1964): 429-31.
15. Davis, R. G. Open market operations, interest rates, and deposit growth. *Quarterly Journal of Economics* 79 (1965): 431-54.
16. de Leeuw, F. A model of financial behavior. In *The Brookings Quarterly Economic Model of the United States,* ed. J. Duesenberry, G. Fromm, L. Klein, and E. Kuh, pp. 465-528. Chicago: Rand-McNally, 1965.
17. Dewald, W. Free reserves, total reserves and monetary control. *Journal of Political Economy* 71 (1963): 141-53.
18. ——— . *Money supply vs. interest rates as approximate objectives of monetary policy.* Washington: National Bureau of Economic Research, 1966.
19. Fand, D. Some implications of money supply analysis. *American Economic Review* 57 (1967): 380-400.

20. Feige, E. *The demand for liquid assets: a temporal cross section analysis.* Englewood Cliffs, N.J.: Prentice-Hall, 1964.
21. Fisher, I. *The theory of interest.* New York: Augustus M. Kelley, 1965.
22. Friedman, M. The demand for money, some theoretical and empirical results. *Journal of Political Economy* 67 (1959): 327-51.
23. ——— . The lag effect of monetary policy. *Journal of Political Economy* 69 (1961): 447-66.
24. Friedman, M., and Schwartz, A. *A monetary history of the United States, 1867-1960.* Princeton: Princeton University Press, 1963.
25. Goldfeld, S. *Commercial bank behavior and economic activity; a structural study of monetary policy in the postwar United States.* Amsterdam: North-Holland Publishing Co., 1966.
26. Goldsmith, A. *Financial intermediaries in the American economy since 1900.* Princeton: Princeton University Press, 1964.
27. Grambley, L., and Chase, S. Time deposits in monetary analysis. *Federal Reserve Bulletin* 51 (1965): 1380-1406.
28. Gurley, J., and Shaw, E. *Money in a theory of finance.* Washington: The Brookings Institution, 1960.
29. Horwich, G. Elements of timing and response in the balance sheet of banking. *Journal of Finance* 12 (1957): 310-44.
30. Johansen, L. The role of the banking system in a macroeconomic model. *International Economic Papers* 8 (1958): 91-110.
31. Keynes, J. *A tract on monetary reform.* London: Macmillan and Co., 1923.
32. ——— . *A treatise on money.* New York: Harcourt, Brace and Co., 1930.
33. Klein, L., and Goldberger, A. *An econometric model of the United States, 1929-1952.* Amsterdam: North-Holland Publishing Co., 1955.
34. Kuh, E. The validity of cross-sectionally estimated behavior equations in time series applications. *Econometrica* 27 (1959): 197-214.
35. Lavington, F. *The English capital market.* 2d ed. London: Methuen and Co., Ltd., 1929.
36. Lindbeck, A. *A study of monetary analysis.* Stockholm: Almquist and Wikesell, 1963.
37. Lydall, H. Income, assets and the demand for money. *Review of Economics and Statistics* 40 (1958): 1-14.
38. Maddala, G., and Vogel, R. The demand for money, a cross-section study of business firms: comment. *Quarterly Journal of Economics* 79 (1965): 153-59.
39. Meade, J. The amount of money and the banking system. *Economic Journal* 64 (1934): 77-83.
40. Meigs, A. *Free reserves and the money supply.* Chicago: University of Chicago Press, 1962.
41. Meltzer, A. The behavior of the French money supply. *Journal of Political Economy* 67 (1959): 275-96.
42. ——— . The demand for money: a cross-section study of business firms. *Quarterly Journal of Economics* 77(1963): 405-22.
43. Miller, M., and Orr, D. A model of the demand for money by firms. *Quarterly Journal of Economics* 80 (1966): 413-35.
44. Modigliani, F. *The monetary mechanism and its interaction with real phenomena.* Washington: National Bureau of Economic Research, 1963.
45. Morrison, G. *Liquidity preferences of commercial banks.* Chicago: University of Chicago Press, 1966.
46. Orr, D., and Mellon, W. Stochastic reserve losses and expansion of bank credit. *American Economic Review* 51 (1961): 614-23.

47. Patinkin, D. *Money, interest, and prices*. 2d ed. New York: Harper and Row, 1965.
48. Phillips, C. A. *Bank credit*. New York: Macmillan and Co., 1921.
49. Polak, J., and White, W. The effect of income expansion on the quantity of money. *International Monetary Fund Staff Papers* 4 (1954-55): 327-52.
50. Riefler, W. *Money rates and money markets in the United States*. New York: Harper and Bros., 1930.
51. Teigen, R. Demand and supply functions of money in the United States: some structural estimates. *Econometrica* 32 (1964): 476-509.
52. Tobin, J. *Commercial banks as creators of money*. Banking and Monetary Studies. Homewood, Ill.: Richard D. Irwin and Co., Inc., 1963.
53. ――― . Money and economic growth. *Econometrica* 33 (1965): 671-84.
54. Tobin, J., and Brainard, W. Financial intermediaries and the effectiveness of monetary controls. *American Economic Review* 53 (1963): 383-400.
55. Vogel, R., and Maddala, G. Cross-section estimates of liquid asset demand by manufacturing corporations. *Journal of Finance* 22 (1967): 557-76.
56. Warburton, C. Monetary velocity and monetary policy. *Review of Economics and Statistics* 30 (1948): 304-13.
57. Whalen, E. A cross-section study of business demand for cash. *Journal of Finance* 20 (1965): 423-43.

UNIVERSITY OF FLORIDA MONOGRAPHS

Social Sciences

1. *The Whigs of Florida, 1845–1854*, by Herbert J. Doherty, Jr.

2. *Austrian Catholics and the Social Question, 1918–1933*, by Alfred Diamant

3. *The Siege of St. Augustine in 1702*, by Charles W. Arnade

4. *New Light on Early and Medieval Japanese Historiography*, by John A. Harrison

5. *The Swiss Press and Foreign Affairs in World War II*, by Frederick H. Hartmann

6. *The American Militia: Decade of Decision, 1789–1800*, by John K. Mahon

7. *The Foundation of Jacques Maritain's Political Philosophy*, by Hwa Yol Jung

8. *Latin American Population Studies*, by T. Lynn Smith

9. *Jacksonian Democracy on the Florida Frontier*, by Arthur W. Thompson

10. *Holman Versus Hughes: Extension of Australian Commonwealth Powers*, by Conrad Joyner

11. *Welfare Economics and Subsidy Programs*, by Milton Z. Kafoglis

12. *Tribune of the Slavophiles: Konstantin Aksakov*, by Edward Chmielewski

13. *City Managers in Politics: An Analysis of Manager Tenure and Termination*, by Gladys M. Kammerer, Charles D. Farris, John M. DeGrove, and Alfred B. Clubok

14. *Recent Southern Economic Development as Revealed by the Changing Structure of Employment*, by Edgar S. Dunn, Jr.

15. *Sea Power and Chilean Independence*, by Donald E. Worcester

16. *The Sherman Antitrust Act and Foreign Trade*, by Andre Simmons

17. *The Origins of Hamilton's Fiscal Policies*, by Donald F. Swanson

18. *Criminal Asylum in Anglo-Saxon Law*, by Charles H. Riggs, Jr.

19. *Colonia Barón Hirsch, A Jewish Agricultural Colony in Argentina*, by Morton D. Winsberg

20. *Time Deposits in Present-Day Commercial Banking*, by Lawrence L. Crum

21. *The Eastern Greenland Case in Historical Perspective*, by Oscar Svarlien

22. *Jacksonian Democracy and the Historians*, by Alfred A. Cave

23. *The Rise of the American Chemistry Profession, 1850–1900*, by Edward H. Beardsley

24. *Aymara Communities and the Bolivian Agrarian Reform*, by William E. Carter

25. *Conservatives in the Progressive Era: The Taft Republicans of 1912*, by Norman M. Wilensky

26. *The Anglo-Norwegian Fisheries Case of 1951 and the Changing Law of the Territorial Sea*, by Teruo Kobayashi

27. *The Liquidity Structure of Firms and Monetary Economics*, by William J. Frazer, Jr.

28. *Russo-Persian Commercial Relations, 1828–1914*, by Marvin L. Entner

29. *The Imperial Policy of Sir Robert Borden*, by Harold A. Wilson

30. *The Association of Income and Educational Achievement*, by Roy L. Lassiter, Jr.

31. *Relation of the People to the Land in Southern Iraq*, by Fuad Baali

32. *The Price Theory of Value in Public Finance*, by Donald R. Escarraz

33. *The Process of Rural Development in Latin America*, by T. Lynn Smith

34. *To Be or Not to Be . . . Existential-Psychological Perspectives on the Self*, edited by Sidney M. Jourard

35. *Politics in a Mexican Community*, by Lawrence S. Graham

36. *A Two-Sector Model of Economic Growth with Technological Progress*, by Frederick Owen Goddard

37. *Florida Studies in the Helping Professions*, by Arthur W. Combs

38. *The Ancient Synagogues of the Iberian Peninsula*, by Don A. Halperin

39. *An Estimate of Personal Wealth in Oklahoma in 1960*, by Richard Edward French

40. *Congressional Oversight of Executive Agencies*, by Thomas A. Henderson

41. *Historians and Meiji Statesmen*, by Richard T. Chang

42. *Welfare Economics and Peak Load Pricing: A Theoretical Application to Municipal Water Utility Practices*, by Robert Lee Greene

43. *Factor Analysis in International Relations: Interpretation, Problem Areas, and an Application*, by Jack E. Vincent

44. *The Sorcerer's Apprentice: The French Scientist's Image of German Science, 1840–1919*, by Harry W. Paul

45. *Community Power Structure: Propositional Inventory, Tests, and Theory*, by Claire W. Gilbert

46. *Human Capital, Technology, and the Role of the United States in International Trade*, by John F. Morrall III

47. *The Segregation Factor in the Florida Democratic Gubernatorial Primary of 1956*, by Helen L. Jacobstein

48. *The Navy Department in the War of 1812*, by Edward K. Eckert

49. *Social Change and the Electoral Process*, by William L. Shade

50. *East from the Andes: Pioneer Settlements in the South American Heartland*, by Raymond E. Crist and Charles M. Nissly

51. *A General Equilibrium Study of the Monetary Mechanism*, by David L. Schulze